DO~IT~YOURSELF
WINE AND
BEERMAKING

Golden Hands Books

Marshall Cavendish
London and New York

GRAEME HARRIS

The Winemaking section was first published in
All you need to know about Winemaking
Cover photographs Graeme Harris
Illustrations Sue Richards

Wine equipment on pages 11, 12, 14, 17, 19, 33, 37,
41, 44, 47, 52, 55, 64-5 supplied by W. R. Loftus Ltd,
1 Charlotte Street, London W.1.
Pictures on pages 6, 11, 12, 14, 17, 19 taken at
Young & Co's Brewery Ltd, Wandsworth High Street,
London S.W.18.

Edited by Alison Louw

Published by
Marshall Cavendish Publications Limited
58 Old Compton Street, London,W1V 5PA
Distributed in the U.K. by WHS Distributors
© Marshall Cavendish Publications
Limited, 1974, 1975
Printed in Great Britain by
Ben Johnson and Company Limited
ISBN 0 85685 110 8
Distributed in the U.S.A. by
The Two Continents Publishing Group,
30 E 42 Street, NY 10017
Library of Congress Card Catalog Number 74-15633

Introduction

It isn't often that you can purchase a wine or beer that suits you perfectly. In fact you could spend weeks looking for a wine with the right amount of sweetness and aroma—or a beer with just the right flavour and body—yet still not find exactly what you want.

The solution is to make your own; in this way your favourite drink is just right every time. And it's not difficult. With a little skill anyone can produce excellent wine or beer, using only simple techniques and household articles. This book explains how. It describes, in clear step-by-step procedure, exactly how to make delicious wine, from the traditional grape or other fruits like strawberry or gooseberry; and beer, from light American-style type, through British brown ale, to dark Irish stout.

It's easy, it's fun, and you'll have the satisfaction of producing something of interest and value using your personal skill—and save money in the process.

The law: Home winemaking and brewing are allowed in most countries but in some a permit is required. The laws differ in minor details from country to country and in the U.S.A. from state to state. If in any doubt check with your local authority.

Measures: Although British and U.S. measures differ slightly, for the purpose of winemaking these differences are small enough to be ignored.

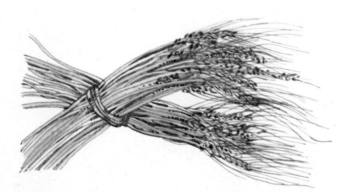

Contents

Beer

Wine

Beer 1 About home brewing

Records of beer-brewing have been found in the areas where the first traces of Western civilization occur, the valleys of the rivers Tigris and Euphrates. The practice of brewing spread steadily westwards via the Egyptian and Roman Empires.

The ancient brew, known as ale, used malted barley as the basic ingredient; the additional flavouring of hops spread from the continent at a later stage. Gradual refinements of brewing techniques gave rise to the popular hopped drink of today. The name ale is, however, still used for certain classes of beer.

Initially beer was brewed in the home, with the finer brews being developed by monastic orders. There has been a recent revival of home brewing as a hobby, and more and more people are making their own beer.

Given reasonable conditions, good equipment and top-quality ingredients (and overlooking the occasional false start), it is possible to improve considerably on commercial products and even develop a brewing repertoire to include lights, through browns, to stouts. One can also produce commendable representations of most local brews at about one tenth of the cost.

Economy

The financial aspect of beer-brewing is, perhaps, the primary attraction to the beginner as the price of beer increases steadily year by year. Although the initial financial outlay may seem large, most of the equipment purchased lasts for several years and after the initial

Oast house used for drying hops.

outlay, the price per pint levels out at only a few pence.

For those with less time and money to spend on the permutations of brewing from first principles, the number of kits available from home-brewing stores is growing every year. These make the task of the beginner much easier and for only a small outlay and very little time a good beer can be produced only three weeks from opening the kit.

Home brewing and the law

Home brewing is allowed in most countries but is usually for home consumption only and not for sale. In some countries you need a permit which is usually free and easy to obtain and sometimes it is forbidden to take the beer off the premises.

The laws differ in minor details from country to country and in the United States of America from state to state. So, if in any doubt, any reputable home-brewer's store will be able to help you.

Types of beer

Home-brewed beer has many variants, of which a few of the more common are listed below.

Lager. This beer originated in Europe and was first brewed in Germany and Czechoslovakia. It has a light, bitter taste with a delicate hop flavour and is pale amber in colour; the head is usually thick and white and 'stays' with the beer for longer than, for example, British bitters. Lager is not an easy beer for the amateur to attempt, as the fermentation conditions are difficult to maintain, being both prolonged and at a lower temperature (45° to 50°F, 8° to 10°C) than for ordinary beers.

Light Ale. A bitter beer which should be light in flavour and clean in taste, with a distinct hop aroma. Light ale should retain a head in a similar manner to lager.

Pale Ale. Originally produced for the British troops when serving abroad. The general consistency of this beer is similar to light ale but expect slightly more body, the starch content being provided by maize or corn and with less hops than light ale. A higher alcoholic content improves its keeping qualities.

Bitter Beer. This name covers a wide range of draught (i.e. in bulk, unbottled) beers on sale today, still with some distinctions as to area, but in general succumbing to the widely distributed 'standard' keg bitters.
It is a heavily hopped beer, made with pale malt, which may vary in colour but which will always have an inherent bitter taste; it contains only a minimum amount of sugar.

Brown Ale. Again this brew can vary greatly in colour, from amber to almost black, but it is a very different beer when compared with bitter. Normally a bottled beer, it is sweeter and more lightly hopped than the beers mentioned so far; this sweetness can vary but there is always a residual sweet taste.

Stout (Irish). This drink is associated with Ireland and in its Irish form has a full bouquet and strong, bitter flavour. These characteristics, and the black colour, are caused by the use of highly roasted barley grains. The head on this type of beer is thick and of a creamy colour.

Sweet Stout. This is basically the same as Irish Stout with the addition of lactose (a

A comparison of colour and head retention of various beers. From left to right: stout, pale ale, brown ale, lager and bitter beer.

sweetener) removing the bitter tang associated with Irish Stout.

Oatmeal Stout. A cross between Irish Stout and Sweet Stout; the small amount of oatmeal added to the brew gives it a distinctive flavour.

Special Beers. These brews are usually heavy in texture and are full flavoured, being slightly more bitter than brown ale. The alcoholic strength is considerably higher than that of other beers.

Mock Beers. As well as the malted beers, there is also a range of mock (or near) beers which can provide interesting variations. These are beers made, for example, from nettles, dandelions and root ginger, which are fermented in a similar way to the malted beers. These near beers have a very low alcohol content as a rule and are generally considered as a 'soft' drink.

Beer packs

The present boom in do-it-yourself methods has created an upsurge in interest in beer making at home. A variety of beer making kits, containing everything except water to make beer at home, can now be purchased. It will pay to study the contents carefully and choose the kits that appear to offer the best value and the clearest instructions. For example, beer mats and labels are inessentials and only add to the price of the kit; look for value in the actual beer constituents.

NELSON HARGREAVES

Beer 2 Ingredients

Beer making is based on five primary ingredients: malt, hops, yeast, sugar and water; then there are a number of complementary ingredients and additives, some of which are unique to individual types of beer — for example, lactose, which is used to sweeten milk stouts, and hardening salts, which are helpful in producing the intrinsic bitterness of bitter beers.

Malt

Yeast feeds on sugar to produce carbondioxide and alcohol. Part of this sugar comes from malt. A number of varieties of malt are available to the home brewer.

Commercial malt. The malt used by commercial brewers is obtained from barley which has to be 'malted' to convert the grain starch into maltose (malt sugar). The barley is spread out on the malthouse floor, then heated and watered until it is about to sprout. During this process enzymes break down the starch. Further sprouting is prevented by drying and roasting the grain. Finally, to complete the process the malt is crushed to form the grist. The grist is then mixed with hot water at 145° to 155°F (62° to 68°C) and kept to this temperature for about 2 hours. This process is called mashing and during this time the starch-to-sugar conversion is completed. The best beers are produced from malt prepared in this manner, but the process is outside the scope of most home brewers.

Malt for home brewing. However ready-malted barley, crushed or uncrushed, is available to the home brewer. Another alternative is to use malt in the form of malt extract, which can be either a dark, viscous substance or in the form of a powder called malt flower. Both the extract and flower are cheap, quick and easy to use and provide very palatable beer.

One of the chief practical differences between using malted barley and a malt extract is that a malt extract brew produces a smaller amount of insoluble solids, thus allowing a higher proportion of the total brew to be racked-off after completion of the brewing. The malt flour, is obtained by grinding the solidified malt extract. It is available in the same grades as the liquid malt.

Hops

Although hops were first used in beer to preserve and stabilize it and not for flavour, their characteristic astringency is now considered one of the most attractive features of beer.

Most good home-brewing suppliers provide a variety of hops for the home brewer. Two main types of hop are produced in English hop fields: Fuggles, which are green and recommended for use with brown ales and stouts, and Goldings, which take their name from their gold colour and are used for the lighter beers and bitters. Imported hops such as Hallertauer or Saaz are usually available for the enthusiastic amateur who wants to attempt the more subtle flavours of authentic, American and continental-style Lager.

These hops are normally available fresh, dried or as an extract. The dried form is most commonly used. If you are using fresh hops ensure that the hops really are fresh; they should be slightly oily to the touch and show no signs of dryness and brittleness. Smell them — the typical acrid hop-odour should be easily detectable.

The only advantage of hop extract over dry or fresh hops is that hop extract produces no appreciable odour during brewing; but better results are obtained using dry or fresh hops.

Yeasts

Almost certainly, the first 'brews' created were initiated by wild, airborne yeast, but nowadays every care is taken to prevent them entering the brew.

Brewer's yeast comes in dried, liquid and fresh

SYNDICATION INTERNATIONAL

form. The most popular is the dried type, usually obtained from the supplier ready-mixed with an energizer which accelerates fermentation. If fresh yeast is used, make sure that it is added to the brew immediately as it quickly deteriorates, even when stored under cool conditions. Do not use baker's or wine yeast for beer-brewing as they are unsuitable and give poor results.

Two types of yeast are commonly encountered in brewing, commercial brewers use a top-fermenting yeast for lights, bitters, browns and stouts and bottom-fermenting yeast for lagers.

Hops, which are climbing perennial plants, growing in Chiddingstone, Kent, Great Britain.

The main difference to the home brewer is one of technique; when using the top-fermenting yeast (saccharomyces cerevisiae) 'skimming' is necessary to clear the fermenting residue from the surface of the fermenting liquid (known as wort). The bottom-fermenting yeast (saccharomyces carlsbergensis) deposits sediment at the bottom of the fermentation vessel and the beer is decanted or siphoned from this. Top-fermenting yeast reacts quickly and produces a good froth on the surface of the wort, which is skimmed off when hardened. Bottom-fermenting yeast reacts at lower temperatures and does not produce anywhere near the same degree of surface activity.

There are two further sources of yeast available to the home brewer. There are a few brands of bottled commercial beer that contain natural conditioning added by the brewer. This is recognized by the fact that a sediment is formed at the bottom of the bottle. To activate this form of yeast, leave the bottle undisturbed for a few days, siphon off most of the beer leaving the sediment undisturbed and add a syrup made up of 5 fl oz (0.14 litre) of water and 1 ounce (28 g) of sugar to the remainder. Shake the bottle thoroughly, then plug the neck with cotton wool (absorbent cotton). The yeast that will grow in the bottle can be used when reasonably active.

Yeast can also be obtained from the second skimming of the wort. Keep it in a glass container plugged with cotton wool (or absorbant cotton) and store it in a cool place. It should be used within one week.

Sugar

Granulated household sugar is the best type for the home brewer to use, being 100% pure sucrose. While brown sugar may have a certain aesthetic appeal it unfortunately contains a number of impurities which can detract from the overall performance of the fermentation and impart slight 'off-flavours' to the finished product. Black malt or caramel can be used to give stouts their distinctive dark colouring.

Fine castor sugar, sugar syrup or glucose is required for priming — that is adding to the finished beer on bottling, to produce carbon dioxide gas, essential for a good 'head'.

Lactose is used in addition when making sweet brown beers and stouts, as this is unfermentable by brewer's yeast and imparts a sweet taste to the brew.

Water

The types of water found in different regions were fundamental in forming the original range and selection of beers brewed, as each region developed its own brew. Some of the best-known breweries started up on the banks of rivers, such as the English Trent with its 'hard' water qualities (e.g. Burton Bitter) and the Irish Liffey (e.g. Guinness) with its 'soft' water. The flavour of the water being considered an essential part of the flavour of the beer.

However, with the ever-present problem of pollution, very few brewers are now able to draw on a clean, private supply for their use. The commercial brewer must use the same water supply as the normal consumer and adjust his formula accordingly.

The domestic water supply is usually perfectly adequate for the home brewing of beer. If the more adventurous brewer wishes to check his supply, then the local water authority can be asked for a detailed analysis. If the water has a low mineral content, the addition of 70 grains (4.5 g) of calcium sulphate and 10 grains (600 mg) of magnesium sulphate per gallon (4.5 litres) will produce the desirable 'hardness' required for bitter beers. Similarly, brown beers and stouts can benefit with 10 grains (600 mg) of sodium chloride (table salt) per gallon (4.5 litres) of water.

Adjuncts

Adjuncts is the technical term for grains used in addition to malted barley, the five main adjuncts being flaked maize, wheat, rice, oats and rye. The main attributes of adjuncts are that they provide a little more body and flavour, but they should never be used in a proportion exceeding ten per cent of the barley or malt content.

Flaked maize (or corn). This gives a drier finish to pale or light beers and can also assist in the clarification (clearing) of the beer. American beers generally contain more maize (corn) than their European parallels.

Wheat. Although used in ale making during the Middle Ages, when it was mixed with the malted barley in quite high proportions, this adjunct has slipped from favour because of its liability to sprout under moist storage conditions, making the control of the malting process extremely difficult.

Rice. This is similar in effect to flaked maize (corn), in that clarification is enhanced; it imparts a slightly drier taste.

Oats. Normally used in the flaked state for the production of oatmeal stout, it gives a characteristic flavour; when using this cereal, ensure that it is fresh and dry.

Rye. Useful in the making of stout. It helps to give a smooth beer with a good head.

Mock beer ingredients

As with wine making, almost any naturally occurring, vegetable substance can be used in beer making and, although the finished product is a good deal different from ordinary beer, it is well worth a try. Typical ingredients commonly used and worth experimenting with are nettles, dandelions and root ginger.

Clarifying agents (finings)

Given normal brewing conditions and assuming that the recipe is followed closely, beer should clear rapidly and naturally. However, if it should remain cloudy it will have to be cleared or fined. The two most effective clearing agents are isinglass, available in both dried and liquid forms, and Carrageen (Irish) moss, a seaweed originating in Ireland. Carrageen moss extract is also available in liquid form.
Isinglass is introduced when the finished beer is seen to be cloudy or hazy before bottling; Carrageen moss or extract is added to the wort about 15 minutes before the end of the final boiling as it is a preventative measure.

Sodium metabisulphite

Sodium matabisulphite is occasionally added to beer when bottling to sterilize and therefore preserves the beer. It is also used to sterilize equipment.
Sodium metabisulphite is obtainable in tablet form—Campden tablets—or as a powder.

Beer 3 Basic equipment

Here is a list of the basic equipment needed. If you are making beer from a kit you will not need items **1** and **2**.
1 Boiling vessel — about 20 pints (12 litres) capacity.
2 Strainer — 9 inches in diameter by 5 inches deep (230mm by 125mm).
3 Funnels.
4 Fermentation vessel — 5 gallon (20 to 25 1 litre) capacity.
5 Spoon with long handle.
6 Siphon tube — about 2 yds (2m) long, $\frac{3}{4}$ inch diameter.
7 Bottles, tops, crown-capping tool.
8 Bottle brushes.
9 Hydrometer — not essential but you must use one for consistent results.

Acceptable materials

It is important to remember when choosing the equipment that the wrong type of material can have an adverse affect on the brew. For this reason certain materials should not be used.
Avoid all metal containers except stainless steel and aluminium. Also avoid enamelled vessels unless they are perfectly sound.
Wooden casks can be used for storage after lengthy sterilization but they should not be used as fermentation vessels.
Acceptable materials for fermentation vessels are hard colourless or white plastic (polythene) and glass. Avoid coloured plastics as some colours are thought to be toxic, particularly yellow. Modern salt glaze crocks can also be used but avoid the old-fashioned type of glazed vessel which has a lead base in the glaze as this can be poisonous.

About the equipment

1 Boiling vessel. This is used for mashing and boiling the wort and is usually a large aluminium saucepan which may hold anything up to 20 pints (12 litres). This type of saucepan invariably has a long handle for lifting and when full of boiling liquid presents a considerable danger, especially if there are young children around. By far the safest and most efficient vessel for boiling is a small, electric boiler with a capacity of around seven gallons (30 litres). The stainless-steel type, rather than enamel, is recommended.

Although such a purchase represents a financial outlay in excess of all other equipment, the convenience and safety make it a sound investment.

A refinement which greatly assists in controlling the temperature during the mashing operation is a pre-set thermostat. If not already built into the boiler a thermostat can be obtained from a home-brewing supplier which is usually set at 145°F (62°C).

2 Strainer. This is used for straining the mash and the wort. Five gallons (22 litres) of liquid is too large a quantity to strain through the normal domestic sieve and it is advisable to purchase a professional caterer's sieve with a minimum size of 9 inches diameter and 5 inches deep (230 mm by 125 mm).

3 Funnels. A plastic funnel about 6 to 9 inches (150 to 230 mm) in diameter is required for filling bottles and a larger one for transferring larger quantities. For final filtration of the beer, kitchen paper is a cheap and effective substitute for filter paper.

4 Fermentation vessel. A choice exists between a glass carboy or a polythene container such as a dustbin. The container must be full when fermentation takes place and a suitable

Aluminium boiling vessel filled with loose dried Hallertauer hops. Also shown are compressed dried Fuggles and Goldings hops, crushed malted barley and flaked barley.

NELSON HARGREAVES

size for the recipes in this book is one with a 5 gallon (20 to 25 litre) capacity. The vessel must be covered with a cloth or an airtight lid to exclude any contamination. A de-luxe version is available with a thermostatically-controlled immersion heater, and is ideal for fermenting beers at the correctly maintained temperature of 70° to 75°F (21° to 24°C).

Polythene or plastic containers are by far the most popular and easily obtainable. They are easy to keep clean and sterile and they are light to handle. As 5 gallons (20 to 25 litres) of beer weighs about 50 lb (20 to 25 kg) this last factor is most important.

Before using the bin, mark the inside in one gallon (4.5 litre) graduations as this saves time during the measuring of ingredients.

If using an old pail it should be first thoroughly sterilized and then lined with a large, un-punctured polythene (plastic) bag to ensure that no contamination occurs.

5 Spoon. A long-handled spoon or spatula is

Assorted stoppers, crown capping tool and labels.

needed for stirring the wort during fermentation, and for stirring of finings or other additives during the final stages of brewing.

6 Siphon tube. A plastic or rubber tube used to transfer liquid from one vessel to another placed at a lower level. One end of the tube is inserted into the top vessel and the opposite end is sucked. When the liquid is flowing into your mouth this end is placed into the neck of the lower vessel. The liquid will continue to flow as long as the liquid level of the lower container is lower than the upper one.

A piece of semi-rigid plastic tubing formed into a 1½ inch long U-bend at one end of the siphon tube leaves any sediment undisturbed and the addition of a hand-operated pump avoids the necessity of sucking the tube to start the siphon action. To close the tube a laboratory clip or a plastic tap can be used.

The end of the tube that is immersed in the wort or finished beer tends to flex about in the fermentation vessel, therefore a foot (305mm) or so of glass tube at this end, again shaped into a short U-bend, makes siphoning easier.

7 Bottles, tops, crown-capping tool. A prerequisite for beer bottles is efficient, airtight closures and bottles manufactured to withstand the relatively high pressure created during the priming of the beer. Exploding bottles are both dangerous and messy.

The most easily obtainable bottles that meet these demands are the ordinary, screw-top, quart (1 litre) beer or cider bottles. But always check the condition of the rubber washer and renew when necessary.

Alternatives to this type of bottle are lemonade bottles with clip-type closures. New rubber sealing rings for the stoppers can be obtained at the home brewer's stores.

The more common pint ($\frac{1}{2}$ litre) crown corked beer bottles can be used with metal crown tops applied with a crown capping tool. When using this tool a useful tip is to hold the bottle firmly in a close-fitting wooden box to prevent it from jerking free as the tool is pressed down.

8 Bottle brushes. Nylon or bristle brushes with semi-flexible wire handles are necessary to clean thoroughly all the inaccessible areas in the equipment.

9 Hydrometer. This instrument gives an immediate indication of the state of the beer with respect to the sugar/alcohol content, and hence the degree of fermentation achieved, by measuring the specific gravity of the liquid in which it is immersed. The specific gravity of a liquid is its density and is compared with the density of water which has a specific gravity of 1.000 at 40°F (4°C).

(For a description of an hydrometer see the chapter 'The hydrometer' in wine section.)

The hydrometer is used with a trial jar. Decant sufficient liquid into the 'trial jar' to allow the hydrometer to float without touching the bottom or sides of the jar. The point where the surface of the liquid cuts the scale of the hydrometer gives the specific gravity of the liquid.

It is the sugar that the yeast enzymes convert to alcohol, so the amount of sugar present is related to the alcohol content of the final product. Sugar dissolved in the wort increases its density and raises the specific gravity. The table below gives the relation between specific gravity, sugar and alcohol. The more sugar that is added to a brew, the more alcohol the yeast produces — 2 oz (57 g) of sugar per gallon (4.5 litres) adds approximately five degrees to the S.G.

It is common practice in brewing circles to omit the first two or three digits and the decimal point when discussing specific gravities, referring to gravities of 70 (1.070) and 6 (1.006).

Type of Beer	S.G. before fermentation	Potential % alcohol (volume)	Amount of sugar per gallon lb oz	g
	1.010	0.9	2	57
	1.015	1.6	4	114
	1.020	2.3	7	199
	1.025	3.0	9	256
Mild, light, lager	1.030	3.7	12	341
Pale ale	1.035	4.4	15	425
Bitter	1.040	5.1	1 1	482
Strong ales, stout	1.045	5.8	1 3	539
	1.050	6.5	1 5	595
'Extra' stout	1.055	7.2	1 7	652
	1.060	7.8	1 9	709
Extra strong beer	1.065	8.6	1 11	765
	1.070	9.2	1 13	822

Beer 4 Additional equipment

Here are a few pieces of equipment that are not essential but may assist the home-brewer:
1 Demi-johns; 2 Cask; 3 CO₂ injector; 4 Labels.

1. Demi-johns. Several glass 1-gallon (4.5 litre) demi-johns are extremely useful when the final stages of fermentation are reached. Used with fermentation locks fitting tightly into bored bungs, they protect the beer from contamination. A second advantage is that they release the fermentation vessel for the next brew. For description of fermentation lock and bung see 'Basic Equipment' in wine section.

2 Cask. An important point to consider in favour of casks for beer storage is that they take up far less room than their equivalent capacity in pint or quart ($\frac{1}{2}$ to 1 litre) bottles. Wooden casks are not really recommended because of the difficulty of sterilizing them and keeping their wooden staves properly swelled and therefore leakproof. However there are many polythene or plastic casks available in a variety of sizes. These are normally fitted with leak-proof tap, carrying handle and a large filler top, so that filling, emptying and cleaning are reasonably easy.

3 CO₂ injector. When storing beer in bulk such as a plastic cask, a useful addition to the equipment is a CO₂ injector. This is a refillable cylinder which fits onto the cask and maintains the liquid, at a pressure above atmospheric pressure, thus forcing the beer out of the cask in the same way as draught keg is served commercially. This improves the head obtained on the beer.

4 Labels. There are a variety of labels that the home brewer can use. Ordinary self-adhesive labels are in common use although multi-coloured labels, similar to commercial labels, are available. When labelling it is always worth adding information that may be relevant to a particular brew. This is a useful way of recording any variations in technique or ingredients employed during brewing.

Pump (which can be used instead of siphon tube), beer stored in demi-john, and Irish moss.

NELSON HARGREAVES

14

Beer 5 Hygiene

Sterile equipment is essential in beer making and it is important to remember that bacteria and wild yeasts are always present in the air around us, although invisible to the human eye. The only sure way to create the sterile conditions necessary is to clean the equipment both mechanically and chemically.

Fortunately the chemical sodium metabisulphite which is used for sterilization is cheap and easily obtainable. Prepare a stock solution as explained in 'hygiene' in the wine section and thoroughly sterilize all equipment including corks, bottles, siphon tubes etc, before use. Soak everything well in the solution and allow to drip dry.

Beer 6 Brewing methods

The basic process

The two methods of home brewing to be described, and the method to be followed with beer kits (which contain instructions), all use the same basic reaction with regard to the formation of the alcohol present in the beer at the end of fermentation.

The raw material which forms the basis of the reaction is starch, provided by the barley; this is harvested and then left in controlled conditions to 'rest' for about six weeks. The barley is then taken to malting houses where, as described, it is watered and heated until about to sprout. It is then roasted to the degree required for the particular beer to be brewed. The degree of roast can vary from a light roast for lights and bitters, to a dark roast for browns and stouts. This roasting stops enzyme breakdown at its peak; the starch is then in a state where the mashing process can convert it into fermentable sugar (maltose) upon which the yeast will act.

The various stages of making beer up to the fermentation stage are all extraction processes. Crushing the malted barley creates a much greater surface area from which the mashing (boiling) process can extract and convert the starch into maltose. After this the wort is stained, three-quarters of the hops are added and the wort is boiled again. This time both to sterilize it and to extract the flavour of the hops. A further sub-reaction takes place at this stage, when the proteins in the liquid coagulate, thus assisting the clearing process.

During fermentation, which occurs as soon as the strained wort reacts with yeast, the yeast breaks down the sugars, converting them into alcohol and carbon dioxide gas. The scummy layer formed during this process is caused by the yeast bubbles and any waste matter present.

Home brewing techniques

There are two main methods of home brewing, other than using a beer kit. The first technique described here deals with the use of malt extract, and the second follows a method similar to the basic process used by the commercial breweries, with malted barley as the basic ingredient. If using malt extract never use more than one pound (454 g) of malt extract per gallon (4.5 litres) of water.

Preparing the yeast

Yeast and yeast starter. When dried yeast is obtained from the supplier it is obviously in a dormant state; the yeast can be added dry at the rate of approximately 1 teaspoon ($\frac{1}{8}$oz or 3.5 g) per 2 gallons (9 litres), although beer yeast is more conveniently obtained in packets or sachets containing the correct amount for five gallons (22 litres). If an extra quick start is required, however, a useful technique to employ is to make a yeast starter.

To do this, sterilize a 2lb (908 g) jar and put in 6 fl oz (170 ml) of tepid water, one tablespoon (14 g) of malt extract and the packet of yeast and a pinch of citric acid. Shake well, plug the jar with cotton wool or absorbent cotton and store it in a warm place for two or three days; after this time the yeast will have gone into vigorous suspension and can be used immediately. The starter can be stored in the refrigerator when not required.

Yeast energizer/nutrient. So that the fermentation process can proceed unabated it may be necessary to add a yeast energizer or nutrient if the yeast does not contain it or if the recipe calls for it; about $\frac{1}{2}$ oz (14 g) per 5 gallons (22.7 litres) causes an increase in yeast activity and hence fermentation. This is particularly helpful in the brewing of the stronger, special ales, which make greater demands on the yeast.

Malt extract process

The chief advantage of brewing with malt extract is the omission of the mashing stage described previously. This means that the smell and trouble associated with mashing is omitted. Malt extract is a treacle or molasses-like substance sold in tin cans or jars. The extract may contain dextrins, to give the beer body, and this point should be checked before starting, as the specific gravity of the beer will be slightly higher than with an extract in which dextrin is absent.

The following method is the general procedure used; variations are detailed in the individual recipes which follow.

1 Put a major quantity of the total water into the boiling vessel and add three-quarters of the hops; bring to the boil and simmer for the specified length of time, adding the remaining hops for the last 15 minutes.

If the recipe includes additives such as maize (corn), or crystal or black malt, boil them with the hops for the full period.

2 Place the malt extract and sugar into the fermentation vessel and strain the hot wort onto

them. Sparge (that is, rinse out) the hop residue with hot water at about 170°F (77°C) and add to the fermentation vessel. Fill fermentation vessel to the volume specified. Add any citric acid required by the recipe at this stage and check the specific gravity. To bring it to the required level add 2oz (57g) of sugar per gallon (4.5 litres) to give an increase in the hydrometer indication of 5.

3 When the wort temperature falls to the required temperature, pitch in the yeast/nutrient mixture, give the wort a vigorous stirring with a long-handled spoon, and cover the vessel with a lid or clean cloth to keep out dust and bacteria. After twelve hours, stir again.

4 Wait until the fermentation has formed a head then skim it off (this does not occur with bottom-fermenting yeast). Top up to the final volume. When a second head forms, leave it to clear itself. A fermentation can be protected from contamination by finishing it in air locked demi-johns. This is a matter of personal choice.

5 Maintain the fermentation temperature of 60° to 70°F (15.5° to 21°C), until the specific gravity reaches 1.000 to 1.010, except for bitters. Stand until the beer clears assisting the process by adding finings if necessary. Siphon into a bottle, filtering if required.

If the lactose is used in the recipe, add it just prior to bottling.

6 After siphoning the beer into bottles prime the bottles with a level teaspoon (3.5 g) of castor sugar per quart (1 litre), or two teaspoons (7g) of sugar solution using 1 lb (454 g) to $\frac{1}{2}$ pint (284 ml) of water. Store the bottles in a warm place for a few days and then move them to a cooler place for final storage.

Malted barley process

In this method the home brewer tries to reproduce the manufacturing processes employed by the commercial brewers. Although this is not completely possible (e.g. the barley used is already malted and dried), the method given here is a domestic representation of this. The quantities used in this method are based on a final volume of 5 gallons (about 22 litres).

The malted barley grains must first be crushed carefully: they must be cracked open but not reduced to powder. It is difficult to do this properly yourself, and is not recommended. Barley already crushed can be obtained and this, although costing slightly more, ensures correct particle size. Crushed barley must be stored in air-tight containers and must be perfectly dry when used.

1 Bring two gallons (9 litres) of water up to 165°F (74°C) in the boiling vessel, remove it from the heat and stir in the crushed, malted barley, malt extract, if required, and any adjuncts; check that the temperature of the resulting mash is about 150°F (65°C).

2 Place a lid on the boiling vessel and insulate it, using old blankets to maintain this temperature for at least two hours. Check the temperature after 10 to 15 minutes, stir vigorously and re-heat if necessary.

3 After the two hours, sieve the mash into another vessel; sparge (i.e. rinse) the grains on the sieve, using six pints of water at 170°F (77°C); add these six pints. Transfer the wort to the boiling vessel, add three-quarters of the hops, bring it to the boil, and continue boiling for about an hour.

4 Add the remaining hops and boil for a minimum of 15 minutes. (If using Carrageen moss, this is the time to add it.) Sieve the wort and sparge the hop residue with two pints (1.14 litres) of hot water; add the spargings to the wort.

5 Allow the wort to cool, then siphon off the wort into a fermentation vessel, ensuring that none of the sediment formed during the preceeding operations is transferred to the fermentation vessel. If the residue is filtered, the last drops of wort can be extracted.

6 Check the specific gravity of the wort and add sufficient sugar to bring the specific gravity to the required level. Two ounces (57 g) of sugar per gallon (4.5 litres) is approximately equivalent to an increase in hydrometer indication of 5.

7 From here onwards follow the 'Malt extract process' from step 3 onwards.

A neatly capped and labelled bottle of beer, surrounded by brewing ingredients.

NELSON HARGREAVES

Beer 7 Trouble-shooting faults & remedies

FAULT	CAUSE	REMEDY
Fermentation slow or stopped	Normally caused by the fermentation temperature being too low	Move the brew to a warmer room (or make the present room warmer) and give the wort a good stir using a long-handled spoon.
Unpleasant smells	Caused by a brew having a top fermenting yeast	Unavoidable. Fumes can be dispersed by uncovering; however this introduces the risk of contamination
Flat beer	Lack of priming before sealing the bottles.	Add priming (syrup or solid) and re-bottle.
	Can be caused by dirty equipment or bottles	Cleanliness in respect of these items cannot be over-emphasized; make sure that only fresh sterilizing solution is used.
	Leaking bottles	Always check the bottle top for cracks and chips and the rubber washers for deterioration before bottling. After bottling, make a final check on the efficiency of the closure by turning the bottle upside down before storage.
Cloudy beer	Insufficient sieving in the early stages or filtering later on	Correct the former by careful addition of finings and the latter by re-filtering.
	Storing the beer at too high a temperature may cause cloudiness	Move it to a cooler environment.
Poor head retention	Can be caused by a a residue of household detergent used for washing the beer glasses	Always rinse the glasses in plain water after washing.
Beer too lively	Often caused by excessive priming	Place in refrigerator for an hour.

Beer 8 Temperatures priming & serving

Vital temperatures

Make sure that the temperature of the wort and/or liquid is always at the recommended level. There are several key temperatures to note during the brewing procedure.

Mashing. The first of these is the striking temperature, which is 165°F (74°C). This is the temperature of the water at the beginning of the mashing process when using grain malt. When the malt is added to water at this temperature, the temperature of the combined ingredients falls to between 150°F and 152°F (65° and 67°C), which is ideal for the mashing process.

Sparging. The third temperature in the sequence is that of the sparging (rinsing) liquid: this should be about 170°F (77°C).

Fermenting. The final temperature to remember is the fermenting temperature. This is the temperature at which the brew will react most efficiently and is 60° to 70°F (16° to 21°C).

Dark beer and lager. These temperatures are varied with two types of beer. Dark beers require a mashing temperature of 146° to 148°F (63° to 64°C) to reduce the dextrin content.

When making lager using the bottom fermentation process, the fermentation temperature must be much lower: the initial ideal is 45° to 50°F (7° to 10°C), and later 55°F (13°C).

Lager fermenting, various beer packs, yeast, sugar, electric fermentation heater which fits into lid.

Priming

Sugar is added to the beer when bottling so that secondary fermentation can take place. The quantity of fine or castor sugar to add per quart, for priming is 1 teaspoon ($\frac{1}{8}$ oz or 3.5 g).

Serving

Beer improves with storage up to a limit determined by experience. If you can resist the temptation to drink it, try storing it for two months; the result is usually well worth the waiting.

NELSON HARGREAVES

Beer 9 Recipes

Ales

Brown ale

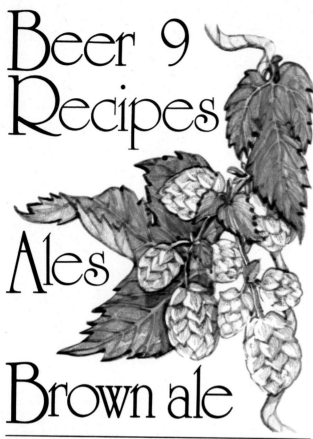

INGREDIENTS	UK/US	METRIC
Malt extract	2lb	908g
Patent black malt	6oz	170g
Sugar	4lb	1.8kg
Hops, Fuggles	3oz	85g
Yeast		
Lactose	1lb	454g

Method

This recipe is for a final volume of 5 gallons (22.7 litres).

1 Add the hops to 1½ gallons (6.82 litres) of water and bring to the boil, reduce the heat then add the black malt. Simmer this mixture for about 30 minutes.

2 Place 2lb (908g) malt extract and 2lb (908g) sugar in a fermentation vessel and strain 6 pints (1.7 litres) of the hopped liquid onto this. Stir to dissolve the extract and sugar and, when dissolved, add sufficient cold water to the liquid to reduce the temperature to 70°F (21°C).

3 Place the remaining 2lb (908g) sugar in another vessel and strain onto it a further 6 pints (1.7 litres) of the hopped liquid. Add this solution to the fermentation vessel and sufficient cold water to cool the liquid to 70°F (21°C).

4 Sparge the hops, strain and cool the resultant liquid to 70°F (21°C) and then add this to the liquor. Continue with this technique until the volume in the fermentation vessel reaches 4½ gallons (20.45 litres).

5 Pitch in the yeast and cover the fermentation vessel with a lid or clean cloth.

6 Place the fermentation vessel in a temperature of 65° to 70°F (18° to 21°C) and allow the initial vigorous fermentation to cease. Skim the yeast head then add sufficient warm water to bring the brew to the correct final volume.

7 After six days, or when the specific gravity is about 1.010, add the lactose (dry or in solution), stirring in gently. Allow the brew to ferment a further two days and then siphon the beer into bottles, leaving 1½ inch (38mm) spaces unfilled.

8 Prime each bottle with castor (fine) sugar or sugar solution. Screw in the stoppers or fit crown tops, then shake the bottle to dissolve the sugar completely.

9 Store at 50° to 60°F (10° to 15.5°C) for about three weeks.

Light ale (malt extract process)

INGREDIENTS	UK/US	METRIC
Malt extract	5lb	2.27kg
Sugar	2½lb	1.14kg
Hops, Goldings	5oz	142g
Yeast		

Method

This recipe is for a final volume of 5 gallons (22.7 litres).

1 Boil the dissolved malt extract, sugar and hops vigorously for an hour in 2 gallons (9 litres) of water then remove the boiling vessel from the heat and stand it in a cool place for about ten minutes.

2 After this cooling period, strain the wort through a nylon sieve into a fermentation vessel and sparge the hop residue twice in the sieve to extract any remaining flavour, using about ½ gallon (2.27 litres) of water for the two spargings.

3 Add sufficient water to bring the total volume to 5 gallons (22.7 litres) and, when the wort has cooled, check that the specific gravity is between 1.030 and 1.034.

4 Pitch in the yeast and cover the fermentation vessel with a lid or clean cloth. Leave the wort to ferment for an initial two-day period in a steady temperature of about 65°F (18°C).

5 After two days, remove the cover and skim off the yeast head, then replace the cover and allow the wort to complete fermentation — in about another five days.

6 The beer can now be transferred to a glass jar fitted with an airlock. Give the beer a vigorous stirring before transfer, then fit the air lock and store in a cool place for four days, or until the beer is clear.

7 Siphon the beer into glass bottles leaving a 1½ inch (38mm) space unfilled, and prime with castor (fine) sugar or sugar solution. Screw in the stoppers or fit crown tops, then shake the bottles to dissolve the sugar completely.

8 Store the beer in a warm place for five days, then move it to a cool environment for final storage. The beer will be ready to drink after two weeks.

Light ale (malted barley process)

INGREDIENTS	UK/US	METRIC
Crushed malted Barley (pale)	7½lb	3.41kg
Sugar (light brown)	1lb 4oz	567g
Hops, Goldings	5oz	142g
Flaked maize	10oz	283g

Method

Follow the generalized proceedure for the malted barley process in 'Beer 6 — methods'. This recipe is for a final volume of 5 gallons (22.7 litres).

Mild ale

INGREDIENTS	UK/US	METRIC
Malt extract	2lb	908g
Patent black malt	4oz	113g
Sugar	3lb	1.36kg
Hops, Goldings	2oz	57g
Yeast		
Lactose	8 oz	227g

Method

This recipe is for a final solution of 5 gallons (22.7 litres).

1 Place the hops in 1 gallon (4.5 litres) of water, bring to the boil, add the patent black malt, then simmer the mixture for about 30 minutes.

2 Place 1lb (454g) sugar and the 2lb (908g) of

malt extract into a fermentation vessel and strain in ½ gallon (2.27 litres) of the hopped solution; stir and add sufficient cold water to reduce the temperature of the solution to 70°F (21°C).

3 Strain a further ½ gallon (2.27 litres) of hopped solution onto 2lb (908g) sugar and add this to the fermentation vessel. Continue sparging until the volume in the fermentation vessel reaches 4½ gallons (20.45 litres), then pitch in the yeast and cover the fermentation vessel with a lid or clean cloth.

4 Place the fermentation vessel in a temperature of 65° to 70°F (18° to 21°C). After two days skim the yeast head.

5 Check the S.G. towards the end of initial fermentation and when it has reached about 1.010 add sufficient warm water to make up to the final volume. Add the lactose (dry or in solution). After secondary fermentation has ceased, about two days later, siphon the beer into bottles, leaving a 1½ inch (38mm) space unfilled.

6 Prime each bottle with castor (fine) sugar or sugar solution. Screw in the stoppers or fit crown tops, then shake the bottles to dissolve the sugar completely.

7 Store at 55°C to 60°F (13° to 15.5°C) for at least three weeks.

Pale ale

INGREDIENTS	UK/US	METRIC
Malt extract	2lb	908g
Crystal malt	4oz	113g
Black patent malt	1½oz	42g
Sugar	4lb	1.82kg
Hops, Goldings	4oz	113g
Yeast		

Method
This recipe is for a final volume of 5 gallons (22.7 litres).

1 Mix the black and crystal malt in 1 pint (568 ml) of water and heat to 150°F (65.5°C).

Retain at that temperature for two hours, at the end of which time boil the 4 oz (113 g) of hops in six pints (3.40 litres) of water for 30 minutes.

2 Add the malt solution to the hop liquid. Rinse the vessel that has contained the malt twice using very hot water and add this to the hop liquid.

3 Simmer the combined solutions for 30 minutes and strain 2 pints (1.14 litres) of the solution onto 1 pound (450g) of malt extract and one pound of sugar; dissolve the mixture and add cold water to bring the temperature down to about 70°F (21°C).

4 Strain a further 2 pints (1.14 litres) of the hop/malt solution onto 1 pound (450 g) of sugar and 1 pound of malt extract, and add to the extract/sugar solution.
When these ingredients have dissolved, add sufficient cold water to reduce the temperature to 70°F (21°C).

5 Add ½ gallon (2.27 litres) of hot water to the hop mixture and strain this into the main solutions, then allow it to cool to 70°F (21°C).

6 Transfer the wort to a fermentation vessel and sparge the hops, straining the liquid into the vessel until the volume is about 4 gallons (18.2 litres). Add the yeast, and cover the vessel with a lid or clean cloth.

7 Leave the wort to ferment for an initial period of 24 hours at a steady temperature of 70°F (21°C). Do not allow the temperature to fall below 55°F (13°C) or rise above 80°F (27°C). Skim the yeast head.

8 After 24 hours, dissolve the remaining amount of sugar in 1 gallon (4.5 litres) of warm water, add this to the wort, re-cover and leave it to ferment for a further 48 hours. Add a sufficient quantity of warm water to reach the final volume.

9 Check that the specific gravity of the beer is about 1.000 after all fermentation has ceased. Siphon the beer into glass bottles, leaving 1½ inch (38mm) space unfilled, and prime with castor (fine) sugar or sugar solution. Screw in the stoppers or fit crown tops, then shake the bottle to dissolve the sugar completely.

10 Store the beer at between 50° to 60°F (10° to 15.5°C) for three weeks.

Special ale

INGREDIENTS	UK/US	METRIC
Malt extract	3lb	1.36kg
Patent black malt	8oz	227g
Sugar	5lb	2.27kg
Hops, Goldings	5oz	142g
Yeast		

Method
This recipe is for a final volume of 5 gallons (22.7 litres)

1 Place 2 gallons (9 litres) of water in a boiling vessel and add the black malt and hops. Gradually raise the temperature of the mixture to boiling point and then reduce the temperature sufficiently to simmer the mixture, holding this temperature for about 30 minutes.

2 Place the malt extract and sugar in a fermentation vessel and strain the hop/malt liquid onto them. Sparge the hop/malt residue with hot water until sufficient water is added to the sugar and malt extract to dissolve them completely.

3 Add sufficient cold water to the combined liquid to reduce the temperature to 70°F (21°C), with an initial volume of 4½ gallons (20.4 litres).

4 Pitch in the yeast and stir the wort vigorously; cover the fermentation vessel with a lid or clean cloth.

5 Place the fermentation vessel in a warm place, maintaining the temperature at 65° to 70°F (18° to 21°C). Allow the initial, vigorous fermentation to cease and then add sufficient warm water to reach the final volume.

6 Allow the wort to ferment for about ten days, skimming off the first yeast head when formed, and then check that the specific gravity is between 1.005 and 1.002.

7 Siphon the beer into bottles, leaving 1½ inch (38mm) spaces unfilled. Prime each bottle with castor (fine) sugar or sugar solution.

8 Stopper the bottles, or fit crown tops, shake to ensure that the sugar has dissolved and store at a temperature of 65°F (18°C) for an initial period of four days.

9 Transfer the bottles to a cooler environment of 55° to 58°F (13° to 14.5°C) and allow to mature for about two months before drinking.

Strong ale

INGREDIENTS	UK/US	METRIC
Malt extract	5lb	2.27kg
Sugar	4lb	1.8kg
Hops, Goldings	4 oz	113g
Salt	2oz	57g
Citric acid	2 oz	57g
Yeast (with energizer)		

Method
This recipe is for a final volume of 5 gallons (22.7 litres).

1 Place the malt extract and most of the hops in a boiling vessel, add 2 gallons (9 litres) of hot water and bring the mixture to the boil; boil for about 30 minutes.
2 Add the remaining hops, salt, citric acid and sugar. Stir the mixture and ensure that all soluble matter is completely dissolved.
3 Strain the wort into a fermentation vessel and sparge the residue with hot water several times, then add sufficient cold water to reduce the temperature to 70°F (21°C).
4 Make up the wort to the final volume, using sufficient warm water to maintain the temperature at 70°F (21°C), and pitch in the energized yeast. Stir the wort and place the fermentation vessel in a warm place at 65° to 70°F (18° to 21°C); cover it with a lid or clean cloth.
5 Allow the fermentation process to reach completion skimming of the first yeast head. Check that the specific gravity is 1.004, siphon the beer into bottles leaving a 1½ in (38mm) space unfilled. Prime each bottle with castor (fine) sugar or sugar solution.
6 Stopper the bottles, or fit crown tops, shake to ensure that the sugar is completely dissolved and store at 50° to 60°F (10° to 15.5°C) for three weeks before drinking.

Bitters

Best bitter (malt extract process)

Bock beer

INGREDIENTS	UK/US	METRIC
Crushed malted barley	7½lb	3.41kg
Crystal malt	1lb	454g
Malt extract (dark)	1lb 14oz	850g
Black malt	10oz	283g
Lactose	1lb 4oz	567g
Hops, Fuggles	4oz	113g
Yeast		

Method
Follow the generalized procedure for the malted barley process in 'Beer 6 — methods'. This recipe is for a final volume of 5 gallons (22.7 litres).

INGREDIENTS	UK/US	METRIC
Malt extract	2lb	908g
Crystal malt	½lb	227g
Black patent malt	2½oz	71g
Sugar	5lb	2.27kg
Hops, Goldings	5oz	142g
Yeast		

Method
This recipe is for a final volume of 5 gallons (22.7 litres).
1 Place the crystal and black malt in 1½ pints

Various ingredients for making beer and the finished product with traditional beer barrels.

(852ml) of hot water and heat at about 150°F (65.5°C) for two hours.

2 Boil 4oz in 6 pints (3.4 litres) of water for about 30 minutes and combine this with the malt solution. Sparge the malt container with near boiling water and add this to the hops; simmer for 30 minutes.

3 Place 1lb (454g) sugar and 1lb (454g) malt extract in the fermentation vessel and strain onto it 2 pints (1.14 litres) of the hopped liquid. Stir to dissolve and add sufficient cold water to reduce the temperature to 70°F (21°C).

4 Repeat this technique adding sufficient hot water at each stage, until about 4 gallons (18.2 litres) of wort is obtained, then add the remaining hop liquid and 2lbs (908g) of sugar.

5 Pitch in the yeast and cover the fermentation vessel with a lid or clean cloth.

6 Place the fermentation vessel in a temperature of 60° to 70°F (18° to 21°C) and do not permit the temperature to fall below 55°F (13°C) or rise above 80°F (27°C).

7 Add the remaining 1lb (454g) sugar disolved in ½ gallon (2.27 litres) of water after 24 hours. Wait a further 48 hours, skim the yeast head then add sufficient warm water to bring the brew to the correct final volume.

8 Wait until all fermentation has finished, then check that the specific gravity is between 0.966 and 1.000. Siphon the beer into bottles, leaving a 1½ inch (38mm) space unfilled.

9 Prime each bottle with castor (fine) sugar or sugar solution. Screw in the stoppers or fit crown tops, then shake the bottles to dissolve the sugar completely.

10 Store at 50° to 60°F (10° to 15.5°C) for three weeks before drinking.

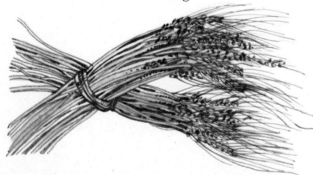

Best bitter (malted barley process)

INGREDIENTS	UK/US	METRIC
Crushed malted barley	10lb	4.54g
Hops, Goldings	5oz	142g
Malt extract (dark)	10oz	283g
Sugar	1lb 14oz	850g
Yeast		

Method
Follow the generalized proceedure for the malted barley process in 'Beer 7 — methods'. This recipe is for a final volume of 5 gallons (22.7 litres).

Light bitter beer

INGREDIENTS	UK/US	METRIC
Malt extract	2lb	908g
Sugar	4lb	1.82kg
Hops, Goldings	4oz	113g
Yeast		
Caramel	½oz	14g

Method
This recipe is for a final volume of 5 gallons (22.7 litres).

1 Place the hops in 1½ gallons (6.82 litres) of water, boil and then simmer for about 30 minutes. Place half the malt extract and 1lb (454g) sugar in a fermentation vessel and strain the hopped solution onto it. Dissolve a further 1lb (454g) sugar and 1lb (454g) of malt extract in 2 pints (1.14 litres) of water, and add the solution to the fermentation vessel.

2 Sparge the hop residue with 2 pints (1.14 litres) of hot water, strain and add 1lb (454g) sugar and the caramel. Dissolve and cool to about 70°F (21°C); combine the solutions and make up with warm water to 4 gallons (18.2 litres).

3 Pitch in the yeast and cover the fermentation vessel with a lid or clean cloth.

4 Place the fermentation vessel in a temperature of 70°F (21°C). Do not permit the temperature to fall below 55°F (13°C) or rise above 80°F (27°C).

5 Add the remaining pound of sugar dissolved in ½ gallon (2.27 litres) of warm water after 24 hours; wait a further 48 hours, skim the yeast head then add sufficient warm water to bring the brew to the correct final volume.

6 Wait until all fermentation has finished, then check that the specific gravity is between 0.966 and 1.000. Siphon the beer into bottles, leaving a 1½ inch (38mm) space unfilled.

7 Prime each bottle with castor (fine) sugar solution. Screw in the stoppers or fit crown tops, then shake the bottles to dissolve the sugar completely.

8 Store at 50° to 60°F (10° to 15.5°C) for three weeks before drinking.

Lager

INGREDIENTS	UK/US	METRIC
Lager hops (dried),		
Hallertauer	3½oz	99g
Crystal malt	8oz	227g
Malt extract	2lb	908g
Invert sugar	5lb	2.27kg
Lager yeast		
(bottom-fermenting)		

Method
This recipe is for a final volume of 5 gallons (22.7 litres).

1 Place about three quarters of the hops in 1 gallon (4.5 litres) of water, bring to the boil then add the crystal malt and simmer the mixture for about 40 minutes.

2 Place half the sugar and half the malt extract in a fermentation vessel and strain ½ gallon (2.27 litres) of the hopped solution onto them and stir. Add sufficient cold water to reduce the temperature of the solution to 60°F (15.5°C) and pour it into the fermentation vessel.

3 Strain the remaining ½ gallon (2.27 litres) of hopped solution and add this in the same manner to the remaining sugar and malt extract. Make up to a fermenting quantity of 4½ gallons (20.45 litres). Add the remaining hops, pitch in the yeast and cover the fermentation vessel with a lid or clean cloth.

4 Place the fermentation vessel in a temperature of 45° to 50°F (7° to 10°C); this temperature is fairly critical and the upper limit must not be exceeded.

5 Wait for the initial fermentation to cease, then add sufficient warm water to reach the final volume.

6 Ferment the wort for eight days, checking the specific gravity daily until an indication of 1.004 or less is attained. When this S.G. is reached, siphon the lager into demi-johns, fit an airlock and store at 55°F (13°C) for up to two weeks.

7 When clear, siphon the lager into bottles, leaving a 1½ inch (38mm) space unfilled, and prime with castor (fine) sugar or sugar solution. Screw in the stoppers or fit crown tops, then shake the bottles to dissolve the sugar completely.

8 Store at 55°F (13°C) for six weeks or longer if possible. Lager should always be served well chilled.

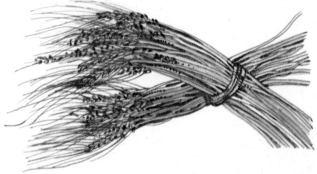

Stouts

'Irish' stout

INGREDIENTS	UK/US	METRIC
Malt extract	1lb	454g
Black patent malt	2lb	908g
Sugar	5lb	2.27kg
Hops, Fuggles	5oz	142kg
Yeast		

Method

This recipe is for a final volume of 5 gallons (22.7 litres).

1 Add the black malt to 1 gallon (4.5 litres) of water and heat for two hours at a temperature of 150°F (65.5°C). Place the hops in a boiling vessel and strain the malted solution onto the hops. Sparge the malt residue two or three times with near boiling water, and add this to the hops.

2 Boil the hop/malt liquid and then simmer for about 30 minutes. Place the sugar and malt extract in a fermentation vessel and strain the hop/malt liquid onto the sugar and malt. Add sufficient cold water to the liquid to reduce the temperature to about 70°F (21°C).

3 Sparge the hop/malt residue with hot water, strain the solution into a separate vessel and cool to 70°F (21°C) as above. Add this solution to the main hopped liquid in the fermentation vessel.

4 Continue sparging the hop/malt residue until the volume in the fermentation vessel reaches 4½ gallons (20.45 litres).

5 Pitch in the yeast and cover the fermentation vessel with a lid or clean cloth.

6 Place the fermentation vessel in a temperature of 65° to 70°F (18° to 21°C) and after the initial fermentation ceases skim the yeast head then add sufficient warm water to reach the final volume.

7 Allow any secondary fermentation to cease and check that the specific gravity is at or below 1.003. Siphon the beer into bottles, leaving 1½ inch (38mm) space unfilled, then prime each bottle with castor (fine) sugar or sugar solution.

8 Stopper the bottle, or fit crown tops, shake to dissolve the sugar completely and store at 50° to 60°F (10° to 15.5C) for two weeks, before drinking.

Oatmeal stout

INGREDIENTS	UK/US	METRIC
Roasted malt	2½lb	1.14kg
Crystal malt	2½lb	1.14kg
Flaked oatmeal	8oz	227g
Flaked maize	1½lb	680g
Sugar (brown)	5lb	2.27kg
Hops, Fuggles	4oz	113g
Citric acid	5oz	142g
Yeast		

Method

This recipe is for a final volume of 5 gallons (22.7 litres).

1 Boil 2 gallons (9 litres) of water and allow it to cool to below boiling point, place the roasted and crystal malts and the grain in a container and pour on the water. Stir the

mixture to dissolve the malts.

2 Cover the container completely with a cloth, and place it in a warm place (65° to 70°F or 18° to 21°C) for about ten hours or overnight.

3 Add the hops to 1 gallon (4.5 litres) of boiling water, reduce the heat and simmer for about 30 minutes.

4 Strain the hopped liquid into the fermentation vessel, and strain in the mash and malt mixture. Add sufficient cold water to reduce the temperature to 70°F (21°C).

5 Stir in the sugar and citric acid and ensure that the ingredients are fully dissoved. Pitch in the yeast. Add sufficient warm water to maintain the temperature at 70°F (21°C) and fill to the final volume required. Cover the fermentation vessel with a lid or clean cloth.

6 Allow the fermentation process to reach completion, skimming of the first yeast head. Check that the specific gravity is 1.003 and siphon the beer into bottles, leaving a 1½ inch space (38mm) unfilled. Prime each bottle with castor (fine) sugar or sugar solution.

7 Stopper the bottles, or fit crown tops, shake to dissolve the sugar completely and store at 50° to 60°F (10° to 15.5°C) for three weeks before drinking.

Sweet stout

INGREDIENTS	UK/US	METRIC
Black patent malt	2½lb	1.14kg
Flaked barley	10oz	283g
Sugar	2½lb	1.14kg
Hops, Fuggles	3 oz	85g
Lactose	10oz	283g
Citric acid	5oz	142g
Yeast		

Method
This recipe is for a final volume of 5 gallons (22.7 litres).

1 Place the patent malt in a container and boil 2 gallons (9 litres) of water separately. Pour the water onto the malt and stir in the flaked barley.

2 Cover the container with a cloth and allow the mixture to stand for 24 hours in a warm room 70°F (21°C). Uncover and strain the malt/barley liquid into a separate container, sparge the residue with hot water, then add sufficient cold water to cool the liquid to 70°F (21°C).

3 Add the hops to 1 gallon (4.5 litres) of boiling water and simmer for about 30 minutes, strain the hopped water into a separate container and sparge the hop residue with hot water, straining this into the container.

4 Add the sugar, citric acid and lactose (dry or in solution) to the combined malt and barley liquid and hopped water, stir the mixture and ensure that the contents are fully dissolved.

5 Pitch in the yeast, make up the brew to the final volume and cover the fermentation vessel with a lid or clean cloth.

6 Place the fermentation vessel in a warm room, maintaining a temperature of 65° to 70°F (18° to 21°C) and allow the brew to ferment to completion (S.G. is at or below 1.003). The first yeast head should be skimmed.

7 When the beer is clear, siphon into bottles, leaving 1½ inch (38mm) space unfilled, then prime each bottle with castor (fine) sugar or sugar solution.

8 Stopper the bottles, or fit crown tops, shake to ensure that the sugar has dissolved completely, and store at 50° to 60°F (10° to 15.5°C) for three weeks before drinking.

Mock beers

Dandelion beer

INGREDIENTS	UK/US	METRIC
Dandelion plants, young and fresh (with root)	8oz	227g
Root ginger	½oz	14g
Sugar (brown)	1lb	454g
Cream of tartar	1oz	28g
1 Lemon		
Yeast (with energizer)		

Method
This recipe is for a final volume of 1 gallon (4.5 litres).

1 Remove any tough, fibrous roots surrounding the central tap root of the dandelions. Wash the plants and tap root thoroughly in in cold water and remove any damaged or diseased leaves or stems.

2 Bruise the ginger and very thinly peel off the tind of the lemon, avoiding the white pith as far as possible (this would affect the final taste of the beer).

3 Place the cleaned dandelions, ginger and lemon rind in a boiling vessel and add 1 gallon (4.5 litres) of water. Boil the mixture/ for about 20 minutes.

4 Place the sugar, cream of tartar and juice from the lemon fermentation vessel and strain the hot liquid onto them. Stir the

liquid to dissolve the sugar and allow to cool to about 70°F (21°C).

5 Pitch in the yeast, stir thoroughly and cover the fermentation vessel with a lid or clean cloth.

6 Move the fermentation vessel to a warm room and leave to ferment for three days. After fermentation has ceased, siphon the beer into bottles, leaving 1½ inch (38mm) space unfilled. Prime each bottle with castor (fine) sugar or sugar solution.

7 Store at 55°F (13°C) for one week before drinking.

Ginger beer

INGREDIENTS	UK/US	METRIC
Root ginger	1oz	28g
Sugar	1lb	454g
Cream of tartar	½oz	14g
1 Lemon		
Yeast (with energizer)		
Campden tablet		

Method
This recipe is for a final volume of 1 gallon (4.5 litres).

1 Crush the ginger in a bowl and mix in the sugar, cream of tartar and the thinly peeled rind of the lemon. Mix the ingredients thoroughly.

2 Boil 1 gallon (4.5 litres) of water and pour this onto the ingredients, stir the mixture thoroughly, add the lemon juice (without pips) and pitch in the yeast.

3 Stir the mixture thoroughly, cover the bowl with a cloth and place it in a warm room for 48 hours.

4 Give the mixture a final stir and then siphon the ginger beer into bottles. Use stoppers to close the bottles.

5 Allow the beer to stand for 24 hours and then ease the stoppers off and allow any excess carbon dioxide to escape.

6 If excess effervescence occurs, add ½ Campden tablet to each bottle. This should

prevent any further carbon dioxide build-up by killing superfluous yeast.

7 Store the beer at about 60°F (15.5°C) and drink after three or four days.

Note Always keep a careful check on the gas content of ginger beer bottles, to avoid dangerous pressurization.

Nettle beer

INGREDIENTS	UK/US	METRIC
Nettle tops (stinging variety only)	1 gallon	4.5 litres
Malt extract (dark)	2lb	908g
Sugar (brown)	1½lb	680g
Root ginger	¼oz	7g
Hops, Goldings	2oz	57g
Citric acid (or lemon juice)	¼oz	7g
Yeast (with energizer)		

Method
This recipe is for a final volume of 2 gallons (9 litres).
Wear gloves when handling these plants. Make sure that the bottles used are strong and in good condition.

1 Select 1 gallon (4.5 litres of young nettle tops; do not use any damaged or diseased plants. Wash the plants thoroughly in cold water. Remove any fibrous stalks or leaf stems.

2 Pour 2 gallons (9 litres) of water into a boiling vessel and bring to the boil. Add the nettle tops and the hops, malt extract and bruised root ginger, then boil the mixture for 15 minutes.

3 Place the sugar and citric acid in a fermentation vessel and carefully strain on the boiling liquid. Stir thoroughly and leave to cool to 70°F (21°C).

4 Add sufficient hot water to maintain the final volume and temperature, pitch in the yeast and stir vigorously.

5 Cover the fermentation vessel with a lid or clean cloth, and move to a warm room. Allow the brew to ferment for three days and

then siphon into bottles. Tie or wire down the stoppers.

Alternatively, allow the beer to complete fermentation and then siphon into bottles, leaving 1½ inch (38mm) spaces unfilled. Prime each bottle with 1½ teaspoon (1.7g) of castor (fine) sugar or sugar solution, screw down the stoppers tightly and store at 55°F (13°C) for one week before drinking.

Spruce essence beer

INGREDIENTS	UK/US	METRIC
Malt extract	1lb	454g
Sugar	1lb	454g
Spruce essence	2½tbsp	35g
1 Lemon		
Yeast		

Method
This recipe is for a final volume of 2 gallons (9 litres).

1 Pour 1 gallon (4.5 litres) of water into a boiling vessel and bring this to the boil. Add the malt extract and sugar and allow them to dissolve.

2 Pour this liquid into a fermentation vessel and add the remaining water; squeeze in the juice of one lemon and add the spruce essence.

3 Allow the liquid to cool to 70°F (21°C) and then pitch in the yeast. Move the fermentation vessel to a warm place, cover it with a lid or clean cloth and allow it to ferment completely.

4 When fermentation has finished, siphon the beer into bottles, leaving 1½ inch (38mm) spaces unfilled. Prime each bottle with castor (fine) sugar or sugar solution, screw down the stoppers and store at 55°F (13°C) for one week before drinking.

Wine 1
About home winemaking

Wine has been made in the home for many centuries and, as commercial wines become more and more expensive, interest in this ancient domestic art is reviving. Excellent wines can be made in the home from virtually any non-toxic fruit, vegetable, grain and flower, in fresh, canned or dried form — even tea or the sap from a tree can be used for winemaking!

Not only is home winemaking very cheap and an excellent way of using up surplus produce, but many people are discovering delicious and exotic flavours which they prefer to the grape. Also, by making your own wine you can evolve one exactly suited to your palate.

For those who still prefer the taste of grape wine, grape juice concentrates have become freely available from the many home wine-makers' stores; with these, commercial-type wines can be emulated. The stores also stock all types of grain, dried and canned fruits and vegetables that are suitable for winemaking, together with all the necessary equipment and additives. The same equipment is used over and over again, so that once the initial outlay has been made only the ingredients are required.

Winemaking and the law

Home winemaking is allowed in most countries but is usually for home consumption only. In some countries you need a permit which is usually free and easy to obtain and sometimes it is forbidden to take the wine off the premises. The laws differ in minor details from country to country and in the United States of America from state to state. So, if in any doubt, any reputable home-brewer's store will help.

NELSON HARGREAVES

34

Wine 2 Contents & theory

Content

Wine comes either dry, medium or sweet, and is a mixture of water, alcohol and flavouring agents — the bulk being water. (In winemaking 'dry' means 'not sweet'.)

The water comes from a tap and the alcohol is formed automatically during the fermentation process. But it is the flavour and aroma that gives wine its outstanding characteristics and which requires the most attention.

Wine can be made from almost anything that can be fermented but it is essential that certain ingredients be present for fermentation or flavour. All the essential ingredients are normally present in wine grapes but with other bases it may be necessary to add certain ingredients such as acid, tannin, yeast, sugar.

Yeast. The bloom on growing grapes is a yeast which is essential to the fermentation of wine. This has to be added to other fruits.

Sugar, which is needed for the action of yeast, is nearly always added. In varieties of grape which ripen late in the season the sugar content is usually sufficient.

So, to make wine, we extract the juices, known as the 'must', from the fermentable material, compensate for any deficiencies in flavour and essential ingredients, add yeast and sugar, and keep the fermentation vessel to the required temperature to encourage yeast action. Care must be taken to keep out any wild yeasts present in the atmosphere, acetobacters (vinegar-forming bacteria) and the vinegar fly. After a short while the must will start to froth and bubble—fermentation has started.

Medieval painting showing vineyard activities in autumn, Castello del Buconcosiglio Trento, Italy.

Yeast and fermentation

When the must ferments the yeast enzymes feed on sugar and convert it to ethyl alcohol and carbon dioxide gas. The yeast continues feeding on the sugar until **a** all the sugar is used up or **b** the alcohol content becomes so high that the yeast is killed and fermentation ceases — this happens when the alcohol content reaches between 10% and 17% by volume.

A deposit known as 'lees' will have formed on the bottom of the fermentation vessel.

If any sugar is left unconverted the wine will be sweet. One way of controlling the sugar is to add only sufficient sugar to produce the required alcohol content and to completely ferment this sugar, leaving a dry wine. Then, if a sweet wine is required, a sweetening agent can be added when fermentation has ceased.

Alcohol content

The alcohol content of wines is normally expressed as '% alcohol by volume'. Most table wines have between 10% and 12% alcohol, equivalent to the 10° and 12° seen on Continental wines. Aperitifs, ports, sherries and dessert wines are usually stronger — between 15% and 30% alcohol. Liqueurs are stronger still — ranging from 30% to 75%.

However, to add complications, there are other ways of measuring alcohol content as, for example, the British proof system, used in Canada, Australia, New Zealand, Ireland and the Republic of South Africa. To make matters even more complicated there are also the US proof and metric systems, the latter named Gay Lussac (G.L.) after its French originator. The following table compares these systems.

	British system	US system	Metric system (G.L.)	% alcohol
Absolute alcohol	175°	200°	100°	100
Normal spirit strength	70°	80°	40°	40
Table wine	17.5°	20°	10°	10

35

Wine 3 Types & usage

Colour

Wines can be red, white or pink (rosé). Usually the colour of the wine will depend on the type of fruit used. However, with grapes it is the skins which give colour to the wine. Red grape wine can only be made from black grapes, the colour deriving from the skins; if the skins are removed as soon as the grapes are pressed a white wine results. Green grapes will produce only white wine. A rosé wine can be obtained from black grapes by leaving the skins in the pressed juice for a short while or by mixing red and white wines.

Types of wine

Wines, both sweet and dry, may be classified as Aperitifs, Table wines, Dessert wines and Liqueurs.

Aperitifs. As their name suggests, aperitifs are intended to stimulate the appetite and to get the digestive juices flowing. They are often, but not always, dry and astringent, with delicate flavours. Sherry is usually drunk as an aperitif.

Table wines form by far the largest category, and quantity, of wine. As the name suggests, these are the wines traditionally drunk at meal times. They may range from darkest red to almost colourless, from sweet to dry, but are usually classified according to colour as red, white and rosé.
All three classifications are produced in different grades of sweetness or dryness.
It is usual to drink a dry or medium white wine with white-fleshed meat such as chicken, fish, veal and pork, while a full-bodied red wine is widely preferred with red meats; rosé wines can be drunk with almost anything.

Dessert wines. These are rich, rather sweet, strongly flavoured wines such as Madeira, Muscatel or Port and are normally taken either with a sweet or pudding course or separately after a meal.

Mead can be made dry or sweet. It has honey as a base and is not to everyone's taste, but make some and try it. Mead can be drunk at any time, before, during or after meals.

Champagne and sparkling wines — the traditional drinks for weddings and celebrations — are bubbling and effervescent. Many home winemakers make very successful sparkling wines. But, before you try, a word of warning: the process of fermentation in the bottle which produces the bubbles can lead to great pressure in the bottles and result in nasty and dangerous explosions.

Fortification

This is the adding of alcohol to a wine either to arrest the fermentation and leave some unfermented sugar, or to give better keeping qualities to the wine, or simply to give the wine a higher alcohol content.
Table wines usually contain from 10% to 12% alcohol. Most aperitifs, dessert wines, Ports, Sherries and liqueurs have a higher alcohol content than this. To increase the alcohol content a wine has to be fortified by the addition of spirits. The home winemaker can use brandy or whisky or a neutral tasting spirit such as Vodka and Polish white spirit for making Port-style wines or liqueurs. The straight-forward fortification of some popular wines is included in the recipes.

Various ingredients and additives for making wine and mead. Note that pale honey is used. These scales are good for measuring very small quantities, such as the small amounts of tannin and citric acid required.

Wine 4 Basic ingredients

Winemakers' kits

If entirely new to winemaking you are strongly recommended to try your hand at one of the several 'winemakers' kits' now available. These kits contain everything needed, except sugar and water, to make 1 gallon (4.5 litres) or 5 gallons (23 litres), of wine. With some kits the container is designed to act both as a fermentation vessel and a storage container, complete with tap. The outlay is not large and the process is so designed that instructions are few and simple.

Wine concentrates

Concentrated grape juices. These include unspecified white and red grape juices and many named varieties including Hock, Burgundy, Bordeaux, Chablis, Chianti, Claret, Sauternes, Port, Sherry and Vermouth. The cans normally contain 2lb 3oz (1 kg) and are sufficient to make 1 gallon (4.5 litres) of wine; larger cans containing up to 1 gallon (4.5 litres) of concentrate are also available.

The concentrates also vary in quality and price. Some mention the country of origin — Spanish, Italian, French; the term 'other Mediterranean' usually means either Algerian, Cypriot or Moroccan, all large producers of excellent wines.

Other concentrates available include apricot, bilberry, cherry, elderberry, peach and various combinations such as grape and bilberry. These concentrates are also sold in 2lb 3oz (1 kg) cans or larger.

Fruits and other wine bases

Canned fruits are available as pieces, pulps and purées, often in 4lb (1.8 kg) cans, or larger. Varieties include apple, apricot, bilberry, blackberry, gooseberry, pineapple, prune and rhubarb. These cans are good value for those who make wines in quantities larger than 1 gallon (4.5 litres).

Dried fruits. Most winemakers' stores carry a good stock of dried apricots, bananas, bilberries, elderberries and flowers, dates, figs, peaches, rose hips, raisins and sultanas (white raisins). Buy the seedless or stoned varieties of raisins and sultanas if possible.

NELSON HARGREAVES

Fresh fruits. The fresh fruits often used in winemaking include apples, bilberries, blueberries, blackcurrants, cherries (morello), damsons, elderberries, gooseberries, grapes, greengages, lemons, loganberries, oranges, peaches, pears, pineapples, plums, pomegranate, quinces, raspberries, redcurrants, strawberries and whitecurrants — the range is endless. Use only fresh fruit as stored (refrigerated) fruit soon loses its flavour. The fruit should be well ripened and, if at all possible, picked on a warm, sunny day.

Fresh flowers. Fresh flowers have been used in winemaking for many years. These include broom, carnation, cowslip, dandelion, elderflower, gorse, hawthorn, honeysuckle, marigold, pansy, primrose, rose petals and wallflower. Gather them on a dry day, when they are free from morning or evening dew.

Grains, leaves, herbs and sap. Barley, corn (maize), wheat and rice are some of the grains used; for the other categories, balm, blackberry shoot, burdock, coltsfoot, fennel, lemon thyme, mint, nettle, oakleaf, parsley, sage, vine shoot, walnut leaf, birch and sycamore sap may be encountered.

Beverages, nuts, spices, preserves. The following may be used: almond, clove, coffee, ginger, honey, malt, tea, vanilla.

Fresh vegetables. Both the more common and more exotic vegetables may be found on the winemakers' shelves: Jerusalem artichoke, aubergine (eggplant), beetroot (beet), broad bean, cabbage, carrot, celery, kohl rabi, mangold, marrow, parsnip, peapod, potato, pumpkin, rhubarb, sugar beet, tomato, turnip. The above list is by no means complete — wine has been made from grass cuttings before now.

Sap and how to extract it

A sweet sap, suitable for winemaking, can be extracted from birch, sycamore and walnut trees in the last weeks of winter while the sap

is rising and just before buds are visible. The extraction procedure is as follows:

1 Operate only on mature trees at least 9 inches (230 mm) in diameter; if the tree is not yours, obtain permission first!

2 About 18 inches to 2 feet ($\frac{1}{2}$ to $\frac{2}{3}$ m) above the ground, drill a $\frac{1}{4}$-inch (6 mm) hole, slanting upwards, about one inch (25 mm) deep, no more, so that only the sapwood is penetrated.

3 Insert a plastic tube, as tight a fit as possible, about $\frac{3}{4}$ inch (20 mm) into the hole. The tube should be long enough to reach into a covered pail firmly supported on, or partly sunk into, the ground. The output of sap is higher than might be expected and the pail may fill in two days. However, 1 to $1\frac{1}{2}$ gallons ($4\frac{1}{2}$ to 7 litres) is enough for a tree to bear in a single year.

4 Strain the sap if necessary; if the juice is not going to be used immediately add two crushed Campden tablets per gallon (4.5 litres) and keep it in a closed container.

5 After the extraction, hammer in a tightly fitting length of dowelling to plug the hole.

Poisonous plants and insecticides

As some fruits and flowers are poisonous, the general rule is not to make wine of any fruit that is not normally eaten fresh, canned or dried. Apart from well known poisonous plants such as deadly nightshade and many fungi, the safe rule is to avoid using any plant unless you have a tried recipe for it.

Beware of picking flowers, leaves or plants that could have been sprayed with weedkiller as some modern weedkillers are highly poisonous. In any case fresh ingredients should always be thoroughly washed before use.

Other ingredients

The other essential ingredients are listed below; more detailed explanations of their usage will be found in the 'Methods' Chapter and, where necessary, in individual recipes.

Yeast. Yeast is essential to any winemaking. Although Baker's yeast can be used it is really

Grapes growing in River Douro Valley, Portugal.

intended for baking purposes; for the best results use a dried or liquid wine yeast specially made for the purpose. Yeasts which are not acceptable are the Brewer's types and wild yeasts whose spores are usually present in the air we breathe.

There are many varieties of cultured wine yeasts — Sherry, Madeira, Champagne, Port, Burgundy, Chablis and Beaujolais — in addition to an 'all-purpose' culture. It is noteworthy that one leading supplier has removed all the named varieties from his catalogue and is supplying the 'all-purpose' wine yeast only, his opinion being that other factors, particularly the grape juice or other main ingredient, affect the flavour of the finished wine to a far greater degree than the yeast, under home producing conditions. However, it is worth trying some of these yeasts to see if you agree. And a cereal yeast is always advisable with cereal wines to deal with the starch content.

Yeast nutrients and energizers. Some grape musts and certain others supply their own acids, nitrogen, salts and vitamins that the yeast needs to feed on. Most other musts are lacking in some of these elements and they have to be added artificially. It is possible to buy yeast nutrient and energizer in a combined form.

Sugar. Nearly all recipes call for the addition of sugar. Ordinary white granulated sugar is normally used. When wines need sweetening after fermentation has finished, lactose, which will not ferment, can be added, but many winemakers use the ordinary granulated sugar for this purpose.

A few recipes call for brown, or demerara, sugar where some stronger flavour is required, but its use is not essential.

Acids. Citric, tartaric or malic acids are required if a wine is to have a well balanced flavour. Some fruits such as grapes and apples usually have enough while other fruits such as bilberries and cherries need some acid added. Citric acid is usually used to make up any deficiency — one ounce of citric acid is equal to the juice of eight lemons and is very

much cheaper. Tartaric acid is sometimes used; it imparts a somewhat harsher flavour than citric acid but some people prefer it in wines.

Tannin is also a necessary ingredient of wine—without it, wines, which are normally slightly astringent, taste insipid. Too much tannin on the other hand, makes a wine too astringent. It is present in some fruits and leaves and in all grape juices. Grape tannin is available in both powder and liquid form.

Pectin destroying enzymes. Some fruits contain pectin, which, although desirable in jam making, causes cloudiness in wine. Depectinizers are then added to the must before fermentation. These are marked under various brand names such as Pectolase, Pectinol and Pectozyme.
Depectinizers inhibit the action of yeast — so wait at least 24 hours before adding the yeast.

Campden tablets. These are multipurpose tablets used for the sterilization of equipment, inhibiting mould growths in must and as a preservative of finished wines. Campden tablets do add a taste to wine but this wears off with ageing.
The active ingredient is sodium metabisulphite, which is also obtainable in powder form and may be marketed under another brand name.
Campden tablets inhibit the action of yeast — so wait at least 24 hours before adding the yeast.

Flavours, spices, herbs

Spices and herbs have long been used to impart various flavours to vermouth and other aperitif wines as well as mulled wines. Ginger is also used in some wines.

Flavouring essences. Special essences, formulated for winemakers, are available for those making liqueurs.

Various stages of wine, from grapes and additives to the finished product.

GRAHAM HARRIS

Wine 5 Basic equipment

The basic equipment needed for home wine-making is extremely simple and costs very little. Some of the articles needed will already be found in the home.

Here is a list of the equipment needed:

1 Boiling container — at least 2 gallon (9 litre) capacity.

2 Plastic pail — at least 2 gallon (9 litre) capacity.

3 Fermentation and storage jars—one gallon (4.5 litre) capacity.

4 Airlock for each fermentation jar.

5 Bored rubber bungs for airlocks.

6 Plain bungs to fit fermentation jars for storage.

7 A siphon tube — at least 4 feet (1.2 m) long.

8 Wine bottles.

9 Corks — for the wine bottles.

10 Corking tool — not essential but a great help.

11 Nylon sieve — at least 6 inches (152 mm) diameter.

12 Funnel — at least 6 inches (152 mm) diameter.

13 Hydrometer — not essential but you must have one if you want consistent results.

Acceptable materials

Acceptable materials for boiling and soaking vessels are: aluminium, stainless steel, un-chipped enamel, glazed pottery and colourless or white plastic (polythene).

Acceptable materials for fermentation and storage containers are: glass, colourless or white plastic (polythene) and, with reservations, wooden casks.

Note: do not use iron, steel, copper and brass as these will spoil your wine. Do not use scrat-

Straining strawberry must. The strainer bag hangs on a metal frame.

ched glazes or glazes with lead in them. Use white or colourless plastic as some colours have proved to be toxic, particularly yellow.

About the equipment

1 Boiling container. Some solids need to be

boiled for a while at the start of the winemaking process.

2 Plastic pail — ordinary household ones, dustbins or garbage pails — the fermenting must is first put in this. The pail should be colourless or white. Choose one with a shiny, hard type of surface.

It is useful to have two of these.

A glass fermentation or storage jar with airlock and bung.

3 Fermentation and storage jars. These are used for fermenting the wine and for storing before bottling. They are usually standard glass jars with two lifting rings on the neck.

Although glass jars are the best they may be difficult to obtain owing to shortages, in which case polythene or plastic containers with screw caps can be used. These containers should be new as polythene often retains the smell of its previous contents. If the container is used exclusively for winemaking and sterilized after use it can be used over and over again.

Wooden casks, if properly cleaned, can be used for storage.

4 Airlock. An airlock or fermentation trap is fitted into the neck of the fermentation vessel and prevents air and bacteria from entering and,

at the same time, allows carbon dioxide to escape. Airlocks are available in glass and plastic. The most popular is a U-tube with two bulbs. The U-bend is filled with water sterilized with a Campden tablet or sodium metabisulphite.

Both glass and plastic airlocks have their advantages. The glass lock has the advantage that the water does not readily evaporate, but, on the other hand, it is fragile and not so easy to clean.

Do not immerse plastic airlocks in very hot water or they may soften and lose their shape.

5 Bored rubber bung. The airlock is inserted through the bung and placed in the neck of the fermentation vessel. Bungs, ready bored through the centre, are available for the storage jars.

The bungs are usually made from rubber or cork. Rubber bungs are preferable as they are easier to sterilize and give a better fit, making an airtight seal. The numerous small cracks and crevices in the cork can harbour a multitude of bacteria harmful to winemaking. Also, these cracks can result in incomplete sealing of a container. If liquid is seen leaking from the sides of the cork during fermentation replace the cork immediately.

Make sure that the bungs you buy fit tightly into the neck of the fermentation or storage vessels you use.

6 Plain bungs. These are used to seal the storage jars after the fermentation period.

7 A siphon tube. This is a plastic tube used to transfer wine from one vessel to another placed at a lower level.

One end of the tube is inserted into the top jar and the opposite end is sucked. When the wine is flowing into your mouth this end is placed into the neck of the lower jar. The wine will continue to flow as long as the liquid level of the lower container is lower than that of the upper one.

If this sounds unhygienic to you, a plastic tube fitted with a simple pump at the opposite end is available and is also very convenient for transferring wine when siphoning is not possible. A small plastic tap to fit onto the end of the tube is another useful addition.

8 Bottles. These are needed for bottling the finished wine. Most wine bottles hold $\frac{1}{8}$ of a gallon (76 cl) but 1 litre bottles — and larger sizes — can be acquired. Remember, wines age more quickly in smaller bottles — the larger the bottle the longer the maturation process takes.

Red wines are traditionally stored in brown or green bottles for a good reason — wines change from red to brown if exposed to daylight. If you can keep them in the dark, the colour of the bottles does not matter so much.

For sparkling wines use specially strengthened champagne bottles for reasons mentioned elsewhere.

9 Corks. A supply of corks or plastic stoppers are needed for the wine bottles. Both should be efficiently sterilized before use, especially the corks.

If bottles are only to be filled for a short while, the flanged type of cork is convenient, being easy to withdraw. These can be used over and over again until they lose their good fit.

Plastic stoppers can be used but it is often difficult to get a good fit. And, when they do fit well, they seal so efficiently that they can be very difficult to remove.

By and large it is better to use the longer, straight-sided corks; they usually seal the best and are the most often used.

10 Corking tool. If straight-sided corks are to be used something is needed to bang them in. The simplest instrument for this is a 'flogger' — a heavy shaft of wood with a flat top which is used to 'flog' the cork in. But accidents can happen and the use of a flogger is not recommended.

A selection of wine bottles.

ALAN DUNNS

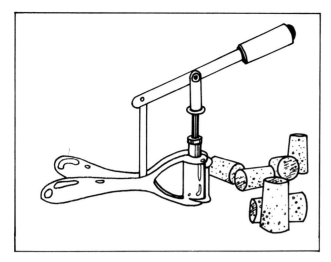

Wine 6
The hydrometer

A hydrometer consists of a weighted glass tube with a bulbous end and a scale along its length. For winemaking the scale goes from .990 to 1.150. Liquid is placed in a trial jar and the hydrometer placed in it. It floats

A corking tool is the easiest to use. There are two or three types available which compress the cork and drive it in with one simple movement.

11 Nylon sieve. This is used to strain the must. Instead, or after, the must can be strained through a nylon filter bag specially made for the purpose. Some types are available complete with frame to hold the bag open, secured to the table edge; otherwise a frame must be constructed at home.

12 Funnel. A plastic funnel, 6 to 9 inches (150 to 230 mm) in diameter is required for filling bottles. It is also used for filtering wines, unless one of the proprietary filters is purchased.

13 Hydrometer. A hydrometer is a most important accessory in winemaking for those not content merely to follow the instructions on the label of concentrates. It measures the amount of sugar present in a solution and tells you whether a must will finish as a dry or sweet wine after fermentation.

In addition it tells you the amount of sugar to be added to the must to give the required alcoholic strength, the potential percentage of alcohol at the commencement of fermentation, and the progress of fermentation — when the hydrometer indicates there is no sugar left the fermentation is over.

Measuring S.G. of finished wine with hydrometer.

NELSON HARGREAVES

44

vertically in the liquid, scale uppermost, the reading being observed where the scale cuts through the surface of the liquid. It is usually adjusted to give correct readings for a liquid at a temperature of 60°F (15.6°C) but, for the purposes of winemaking, the readings are sufficiently accurate if the temperature of the liquid varies between 51°F and 69°F (10.6°C and 20.6°C).

How it works

The measurement taken is the specific gravity (S.G.) of the must or wine. (The S.G. of pure water is 1.000 and readings are relative to water.) The more sugar there is dissolved in the wine the denser the wine will be and the higher the hydrometer will float. When the sugar is entirely converted to alcohol, which is less dense that water, the hydrometer will sink down further and read, possibly, .990.
Thus the hydrometer, which is used in a long, narrow 'trial jar', can be used for determining:
1 The S.G. (and hence the sugar content) of the must before fermentation.
2 The amount of sugar to be added to the must to give the required alcoholic strength.
3 The potential percentage of alcohol at the commencement of fermentation.
4 The progress of fermentation.
5 The actual percentage of alcohol at the conclusion of fermentation.
To determine whether a must will produced a dry or sweet wine here is a guide for the reading:
Dry   —1.088 to 1.095
Medium —1.110 to 1.130
Sweet   —1.135 to 1.150
The specific gravities of the actual wine, when fermentation has ceased is:
Dry wine: .085 to .990
Medium wine: .990 to 1.001
Sweet wine: 1.001 to 1.005

The hydrometer and alcohol content

It is sugar that the yeast enzymes convert to alcohol, so the amount of sugar present is related to the alcohol content of the final product. (But do remember that after a certain percentage of alcohol is present in the liquid, about 10% to 17% by volume, the yeast is killed and further fermentation brought to a halt. Any remaining sugar stays unconverted and goes to produce a sweet wine.)
The hydrometer reading of the must suggests the amount of sugar still needed to produce the required alcohol content.
If a hydrometer reading is taken initially a further reading will indicate the progress of fermentation.
The table shows the potential % alcohol that should be obtained for a certain S.G.

For a must of a specific S.G. the amount of sugar already present and the potential % of alcohol is as follows, per gallon (4.5 litres).

S. G.	Sugar already present			Potential % alcohol	S. G.	Sugar already present			Potential % alcohol
	lb	oz	kg			lb	oz	kg	
1.040		13	.36	5.4	1.085	1	15	.879	11.4
1.045		15	.42	6.1	1.090	2	1	.936	12.1
1.050	1	1	.48	6.8	1.095	2	3	.992	12.8
1.055	1	3	.53	7.4	1.100	2	5	1.05	13.4
1.060	1	5	.59	8.1	1.105	2	7	1.11	14.1
1.065	1	7	.65	8.8	1.110	2	9	1.16	14.7
1.070	1	9	.70	9.5	1.115	2	11	1.22	15.4
1.075	1	11	.76	10.1	1.120	2	13	1.28	16.0
1.080	1	13	.82	10.8	1.125	2	15	1.33	16.8

It will be noticed that for every two ounces of sugar added to the must, its S.G. rises by .005 and its potential alcohol by approximately 0.65%. These are useful figures to remember.

Wine 7 Additional equipment

1 Boiler, 2 Filter, 3 Labels, 4 Liquidizer or blender, 5 Measuring jug, 6 Mashers and spoons, 7 Press, 8 Safety lock.

1 Boiler. If you intend to make wine in large quantities and the recipe calls for boiling the pulp a small electric boiler will make life a lot easier and safer; it is difficult for some people to lift five gallons (23 litres) of boiling mash from the top of a cooker.

2 Filter. Sometimes a wine will not clear and needs to be fined or filtered. A number of proprietary filters are available, one incorporating a force pump that enables filtering to be completed in a few minutes. There are also a number of filtering and fining materials that enable wine to be cleared of all cloudiness or haze.

3 Labels. You can add a professional touch to your bottles with some of the many colourful wine labels which are sold in packets. Better still, have your own printed. In any case, even if the label is just plain, all wine you make should be carefully labelled with contents and date of bottling.

4 Liquidizer or blender. A liquidizer or blender is excellent for preparing ingredients for wine must. If you have a lot of fruit to mince (grind) or purée you will find it a slow process with a mincer or a liquidizer of the smallest household type. The larger professional models, that will also slice and grate, are a better investment.

5 Measuring jug. A one litre glass or plastic measuring jug is very useful.

6 Mashers and spoons. These are handy items for breaking down soft ingredients — the ordinary potato masher with slots is ideal, but choose the stainless steel type. Large stainless steel spoons are also useful, but wooden spoons can be used instead if well sterilized before use.

7 Press. A press is a device for extracting the maximum amount of juice from the fruit or pulp. If you make a lot of wine and in large quantities, a press is useful to have provided you have space to store it.

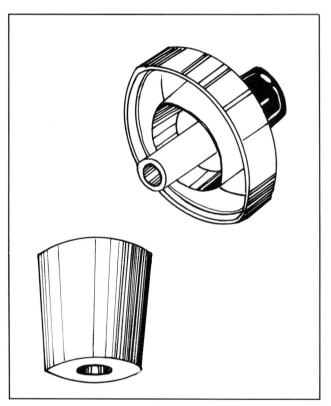

8 Safety lock. The safety lock, or dry fermentation lock, is an excellent device to close the storage container if there is any doubt as to whether or not fermentation has finished completely, and as a precaution in case it restarts.

Two or three types are available to fit 1 gallon (4.5 litre) containers. One sort, using an enclosed steel ball to maintain the seal, has a stem of the same size as an airlock so it can be inserted into a bored rubber bung and then into the container, thus ensuring a better seal than the all-plastic type.

Wine 8 Hygiene

Hygiene is of the utmost importance in wine-making. Fortunately the chemical sodium metabisulphite which is used for sterilization is cheap and easily obtainable. It serves also as an anti-oxidant in the must and as a preservative for finished wine.

Sodium metabisulphite is obtainable in tablet form, known as Campden tablets, or as a powder. The tablets, crushed, are very convenient to add to the must or the finished wine, but a stock solution made from the powder is easier for the sterilization of equipment. Sodium metabisulphite needs an acid medium for effective results.

Sterilizing bottles, corks and corker.

Making a stock solution

To make a stock solution, dissolve $1\frac{1}{2}$ oz (43 g) of the powder with $\frac{1}{8}$ oz (3.5 g) of citric acid in 1 gallon (4.5 litres) of warm water. Caution — do not inhale the fumes.

If, for any reason, sodium metabisulphite powder is difficult to obtain, 7 or 8 crushed Campden tablets equal approximately $\frac{1}{2}$ oz (14 g) of the powder.

Thoroughly rinse or soak everything in the solution: buckets, siphon tube, bottles, etc. Do not rinse them in fresh water but allow everything to drip dry. The same sterilization rules also apply to corks, bungs, stoppers and airlocks. Soak these items well in the solution before use.

If the solution is stored in a closed container it can be used over and over again until the fumes are no longer apparent.

Wooden casks

Wooden casks are not often seen these days, but if you get hold of one and want to use it for storing wine special care care must be taken to thoroughly clean and sterilize it.

First, if it has dried out it must be filled with water to which a quantity of stock solution has been added, and allowed to soak well until the wood has swollen and all leaks have disappeared. Next, empty it out and fill with very hot water to which washing soda or lime has been added. Partly empty it and go over the entire inside with a long stiff brush. Empty it again and if much debris comes away repeat the brushing until it is clean.

When there is no trace of a musty or sour odour coming from the cask it can be considered safe. Rinse it out once or twice more with the sterilizing solution and allow to drain.

Bottles

A good way of cleaning encrusted bottles is with about 3 feet (1 m) of metal chain such as is used for bath plugs. Put a little water in the bottle, drop in most of the chain and swirl it about vigorously. Alternatively use a nylon or bristle brush on a wire handle.

Wine Methods 9

Each recipe gives detailed step by step instructions on how to make wine. However here are the various procedures to give you an idea of the processes.

Preparation of wine musts

If you are using canned grape juice concentrates for your winemaking the work has all been done for you, and this section can be ignored. The next that concerns you is 'Adding the sugar'.

Various methods of must preparation are required according to the ingredients used. The basic principles are given below but any special requirements will be noted in the individual recipes.

Ingredient	Preparation required
Root vegetables	Boil for long enough to soften the material, but do not overcook or the flavour will be lost. Mash and press or place in a liquidizer or blender if preferred.
Berries and soft fruit, except grapes	Pour nearly boiling water over fruit to cover. Leave for two or three days until mushy.
Grapes	Press out the juice; soaking is not required.
Apples, pears	Chop up and soak in cold water for two or three days with one crushed Campden tablet. Press, liquidize or blend.
Canned fruits, fresh stone fruits	Pour nearly boiling water over the fruit to cover.

Dried fruits   Remove raisin or sultana seeds, then chop up or mince (grind) before adding to the must.

Old Roman mosaic shows grapes being trampled.

The juice is not extracted immediately after the above preparation in every instance: sometimes yeast and sugar are added to the pulp which is then allowed to ferment before juice extraction, as set out in individual recipes.

When the pulp is to be fermented in this way it is placed in a container closed to bacteria, flies and wild yeasts, but open to the air. The plastic pail should be covered with a piece of fabric sheeting or 5 to 6 layers of muslin or cheese cloth. Do not use plastic sheeting as this will prevent air getting to the must.

This is called the aerobic fermentation period. After this the must is transferred to a nylon filter bag suspended over a plastic pail for the juice to drain into. Coarse particles may first be removed by passing the pulp through a semi-rigid nylon strainer.

Complete extraction may take a day or less, depending on the proportion of juice to solid matter remaining. With some strongly flavoured fruits, such as elderberries or blackcurrants, one or two pints of hot water poured into the bag will flush out more juice, but do not overdo this second process. Except with parsnips, you can squeeze the bag to hasten the process and obtain more juice.

Preparation of mead musts

Honey — the main ingredient of mead — must be sterilized to destroy bacteria and mould spores before fermentation. The only certain way is to add water to the honey and bring the mixture to the boil, but if fruit or juices are to be added, boil the honey first and separately, otherwise unwanted pectin may be extracted from the fruit.

Crushed Campden tablets can be used as an

49

Preparing grapes for pressing. The traditional trampling has been largely abandoned.

SUSAN GRIGGS AGENCY/JOHN GARRETT

alternative to boiling but their action is not so powerful.

Adding the sugar

The next stage is to add the sugar. Most wine-makers seem to follow the practice of adding all the sugar at one time and most of the recipes therefore call for this to be done. However, it is often beneficial to split the sugar into two or even more portions, and add these in stages.

Other additions

Pectin destroying enzymes, available in liquid or powder form, are added, if required, when the must is cool and 24 hours before the addition of the yeast.
The amount to be added depends on the brand, so follow the instructions on the label.

Tannin. Without tannin wines taste insipid. Bilberries, elderberries, grapes, oakleaves, tea and unpeeled pears all have adequately high tannin content for winemaking, but most other substances call for its addition. However, a small quantity makes a big difference as too much can make the wine very astringent. So if you are going to add tannin be cautious at first, adding less rather than more, and refine the quantity next time.
Grape tannin comes in a fine powder or liquid form. Tannin in powder form does not mix easily, so mix into a thin paste first with a small amount of water before adding.

Here is a suggestion for the amounts needed per gallon (4.5 litres) of wine:
For white wines $\frac{1}{16}$ oz (1.75 g) of powder or 2 to 3 drops of liquid.
For red wines $\frac{1}{8}$ oz (3.5 g) of powder or 4 to 6 drops of liquid.

Tea can be used as an alternative to tannin.

50

A teaspoon (5 ml) of strong infused tea per gallon of must is suggested.

Citric acid is usually added for a well balanced flavour when the base ingredient lacks it. Amounts vary from $\frac{1}{4}$ to $\frac{1}{2}$ oz (7 to 14 g) per gallon. The crystals dissolve easily and are stirred into the must.

Tartaric acid is sometimes added instead of citric acid where a harsher flavour is required. Use in the same quantities as tannin.
When potassium salts are present in the wine the tartaric acid and salts combine to form crystals, but these crystals can be easily removed by refrigerating the wine and racking off into a clean container.

Precipitated chalk. Very acid musts, such as those made from rhubarb, can have their acidity reduced by sprinkling $\frac{1}{2}$ oz (14 g) of precipitated chalk into a gallon (4.5 litres) of must before fermentation. More than this quantity will spoil the flavour. As the action of the chalk develops, the wine will fizz considerably; when it has died down fermentation in the usual way may be commenced.

Glycerine is a natural by-product of wine. Its addition in small quantities — $\frac{1}{8}$ fl oz (3.5 ml) per bottle — can enhance a rough wine, reducing harshness and generally improving the flavour.

Campden tablets, sometimes added to the must to prevent unwanted bacterial action and moulds forming, should be added 24 hours before adding the yeast. Use one crushed tablet per gallon (1.45 litres) of must.

Yeast and starter bottles

To start fermentation yeast must be added together with a nutrient.

Quantities. The amount of yeast per gallon (4.5 litres) is usually one tablet, small bottle or packet of wine yeast and about $\frac{1}{8}$ oz (3.5 g) of granulated yeast. For yeast nutrient use $\frac{1}{8}$ oz (3.5 g) per gallon (4.5 litres) or as directed on the label of the container.

Too much yeast causes rapid fermentation, but may leave a yeasty flavour in the finished wine. This 'off' flavour may persist for a few months but usually disappears with time. Too little yeast may take a long time to get going, or may not start at all.

Starter bottle. Granulated yeast usually starts fermentation off almost immediately, but some of the special wine culture yeasts require activating separately in a 'starter bottle' before addition to the must.
To prepare a starter bottle add the yeast, nutrient, 1 oz (28 g) of sugar, a pinch of citric acid and $\frac{1}{4}$ pint (142 ml) of water (or according to the directions supplied with the yeast) at 77°F (25°C) to a small bottle. Shake thoroughly, plug the bottle with cotton wool (absorbent cotton). Keep the bottle warm about 24 hours. When the yeast is working actively add it to the must. A starter bottle will often get a must fermenting when addition of yeast directly to the must will not.

Temperature and yeast action. The correct temperature is most important to the action of the yeast. If the temperature gets too low (under 50°F or 10°C) fermentation will slow down or stop. If it gets too high (over 90°F or 32°C) the yeast will die.
The temperature during the aerobic fermentation period (while the pail is covered with a cloth) should be about 70°F (21°C).
During the anaerobic fermentation period (when the fermentation vessel is sealed with an airlock) the temperature should be about 65°F (18°C).

Fermentation progress

As the yeast starts to work considerable bubbling and frothing occurs. The must will change to a milky colour as the yeast grows. It is a good idea, if the working area is confined, to place a sheet of newspaper around the fermentation container to avoid damage to wallpaper and surroundings.
When the must has been transferred to the fermentation jar keep an eye on the airlock for

the first few days to make sure there is always water present to maintain the trap; evaporation and spillage may necessitate topping up daily. After this initial activity has slowed down the container can be removed to a cooler place, but preferably not below about 62°F (17°C). Fermentation will gradually decrease and, after about four or five weeks, the line of bubbles around the top of the container will have died away completely — if not, wait another few days to make sure that no gas is being given off.

Racking

Dead yeast and perhaps other solid matter (the 'lees') have by now settled at the bottom of the fermentation jar. If left there, an unpleasant

flavour may be imparted to the wine, which it has now become, and so they should be removed. To do this the wine has to be siphoned into a second sterilized container with a siphon tube or pump. You can stand the wine container on a table and set the second container on the floor. Care should be taken that the tube is clear of the sediment.

This process is called racking the wine.

The lower container should be topped up, if necessary, with cooled boiled water as it is preferable to have the minimum of air space remaining.

Crush one Campden tablet per gallon (4.5 litres) of wine and add before sealing the container with a solid bung or safety lock; these tablets act as a preservative and help to stop further fermentation.

Store in a cool, dry place.

Rack off the wine into a clean container every eight weeks or so, to remove sediment till the wine becomes clear.

Bottling

When the wine has become clear, and then only, it is ready to be bottled. Do not be disappointed if the flavour of the wine at this time does not meet your expectations; it may taste 'yeasty'. The flavour and aroma will improve as the wine is stored — two months for some wines, two years for others.

If the wine does not clear it will need to be fined or filtered.

For each gallon of wine you will need six sterilized bottles and corks. Siphon or pump the wine into them until full, then fit corks or stoppers according to your chosen method. And don't forget to label the bottles before putting them away.

Most winemakers also find it useful to keep a record of their activities — the ingredients of the must, the type of yeast used, the quantity of sugar and when added, other additives, S.G. at various stages and comments on the end results. Such information is very useful for guidance in another year and essential if you want to improve your winemaking.

Racking wine into bottles.

Wine 10 Maximum strength & other wines

Maximum strength wines

To produce wines with an alcohol content above 13%, ever increasing care and nursing is required. Although the activity of most yeasts is inhibited at around 17% alcohol, wines of up to 21% can be produced.

These are the points to watch:

1 Prepare a must with a high fruit content by doubling the quantity of the recipe.

2 Use the correct wine culture yeast — both the Sherry and Tokay types are recommended for high alcoholic strength wines.

3 Maintain the supply of yeast nutrient and vitamins when adding sugar.

4 Keep the temperature correct — 70°F (21°C), or as specified by the directions supplied with the particular yeast.

5 Keep the temperature constant — a thermostatically controlled heater, inserted in the fermentation jar, is available for this purpose.

6 Feed the sugar in gradually, in perhaps six or seven portions, instead of two or three.

Sparkling wines

Sparkling wines are produced by inducing a secondary fermentation within a sealed bottle. This is an advanced process and a first requirement is a number of proper champagne bottles which are specially strengthened — ordinary bottles are not strong enough to withstand the gas pressure developed within. Burst bottles are dangerous! And a word of warning — accidents can still happen.

The true champagne method is lengthy,

requiring at least a year of skilled attention to each bottle, and is unlikely to appeal to the amateur. However, it is possible to make a sparkling wine — that is a wine that is still fermenting slightly, therefore still giving off carbon dioxide gas from the yeast. The French call this state 'petillanté'.

Select a light coloured white wine. Before fermentation has quite finished, rack the wine, but allow a little sediment to rise. Then pour into champagne bottles, leaving room for a syrup made of 2 oz (57 g) of sugar in each bottle. After adding the sugar close securely and wire down the stoppers—the plastic stoppers are best here.

Stand the bottles upright in a warm place (70°F, 21°C), watching them carefully. When a new fermentation is seen to start remove the bottles to cooler surroundings of about 60°F (15.5°C), and leave them for at least nine months.

Open and pour very carefully to avoid disturbing the sediment.

Liqueurs

To make liqueur, use a wine without a strong flavour, since a flavouring agent is added. To fortify the wine a flavourless spirit is required — Polish Vodka, Vybora, is commonly added; this Vodka is obtainable in 100° and 140° proof spirit strengths. Quantities are given below for both strengths.

Having chosen the flavour required, put $\frac{1}{8}$ fl oz (3.5 ml) of the liqueur essence into an ordinary wine bottle, then add 6 oz (170 g) of sugar dissolved in a little hot water. Add the Vodka according to the table below, then fill with the wine; cork securely. No fermentation is involved and the liqueur will be ready in a few days.

Vodka added per bottle				Resultant
100° proof		140° proof		liqueur strength
fl oz	ml	fl oz	ml	proof
3	85	2	56	40°
6	170	4	114	50°
9	256	5	142	60°

Instant wines

So-called 'instant' wines, ready for drinking within a few weeks of starting fermentation, can be produced by the use of concentrates or other light-bodied basic materials, reducing the sugar content, using granulated, quick-acting yeast, and repeated filtering. Such wines will have a low alcoholic content, say 7° to 8°, but are pleasant drinks in the warmer weather. They will not keep for long.

Wine 11 Fining & filtering

If the wine does not clear about two months after the initial racking (or longer if indicated in the recipe), it can be cleared either by fining of filtering. Filtering is usually tried first and if that fails it should be fined. However, some people prefer the Bentonite fining powder to any other method.

Filtering

The filtering agents that may be used are proprietary filters, cellulose powder and

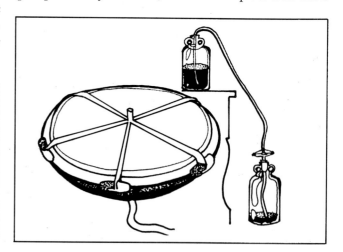

diatomaceous silica.

It should be noted that there is some doubt about the advisability of using asbestos powder (although it is still available in some areas) for reasons of health.

The proprietary filters are efficient and very simple to use. Full instructions are supplied with the filter.

For all other methods you will need a plastic funnel about 6 to 9 inches in diameter (150 to 230 mm), some good quality cotton wool (absorbent cotton), and a support for the funnel. (The support can easily be made from a 12 inch (300 mm) square of hardboard with a 4 inch (100 mm) hole cut in the centre, with both sides covered in thin self-adhesive plastic sheeting for easy cleaning.)

Plug the stem of the funnel with cotton wool, packing it down fairly tightly. Sprinkle in a layer of loose-packed cellulose powder or diatomaceous silica, about $\frac{3}{4}$ inch (20 mm) deep. Fill the funnel with wine. At first the powder will tend to float but will gradually settle down. If the wine does not clear pass this first quantity back through the funnel, pouring the wine gently down the side of the funnel so that the filter layer is disturbed as little as possible. If the wine clears proceed to filter the rest. If it does not clear the wine will have to be fined. After a gallon (4.5 litres) has passed through, or if the filtering rate has become too slow, renew the cotton wool and filter medium.

Fining

If filtering does not clear the wine it will have to be fined. The fining agents that may be used are isinglass, egg white, egg shell, proprietary finings or Bentonite.

It is easier to fine wine when it is in bulk rather than in a bottle.

First rack off the wine if there is any sediment into a clean jar.

After initial preparation of the chosen fining ingredients (see below) the fining agent is added to the wine, left from four to six days to clear

Wine being filtered to remove suspended particles in the wine.

the wine, then the wine is carefully racked off into a clean jar or bottles, taking care not to disturb the sediment.

Eggshells. Clean them and bake in an oven until brittle. Crush them into a coarse powder. Sprinkle into the wine, using $\frac{1}{2}$ oz (14 g) to each gallon (4.5 litres).

Egg white. Discard the yolk, pour off up to a pint of the wine and beat the white into this wine — an electric mixer is helpful.
Add the mixture to the bulk of the wine. One egg white will fine 5 gallons (23 litres).

Isinglass and proprietary finings. Pour in a measured quantity, about $\frac{1}{2}$ fl oz (14 ml) per gallon (4.5 litres) or as directed on the label, and stir thoroughly.

Bentonite powder is a fine clay powder which swells in water forming sticky particles which appear to absorb all the haze and cloudiness as they sink to the bottom. It is strongly recommended as a cleaning agent and usually succeeds where some of the other agents only do half the job.
Add $\frac{3}{4}$ oz (21 g) of the Bentonite powder to $\frac{3}{4}$ pint (426 ml) of cold water in a pint (568 ml) size bottle. Shake the bottle really vigorously until all the powder has gone into suspension and there is none left sticking to the sides or bottom. Stand the bottle for about a day, shaking occasionally, and it will be found that the powder no longer tends to settle.
It can now be added to the wine — about $\frac{1}{4}$ fl oz (7 ml) to a bottle or 1 to $1\frac{1}{2}$ fl oz (28 to 42 ml) per gallon (4.5 litres) of wine.
Agitate the wine several times during the first day, then leave it for five or six days, when it should be perfectly clear. Decant or rack the wine carefully, as the sediment is very light.
Bentonite gel is also available. This can be added directly to the wine and merely stirred a few times to disperse it; racking should follow in a few days. Add 8 oz (227 g) per gallon (4.5 litres) of wine.
Note. Do not add more Bentonite than stated above or it may spoil the flavour of the wine — the correct amount will not affect it.

Wine 12 Controlling the sugar

Each recipe suggests quantities of sugar to be added and the resulting type of wine — dry, sweet, medium. If you want to adjust this to your own taste, making a wine sweeter or drier, it is advisable to add the sugar in stages and to use a hydrometer. Apart from this, the procedure for making the wine is the same as the recipe.
One way of making medium to sweet wines is to first make a dry one and then, after fermentation has stopped, to add sugar to your taste.

Grape juice concentrates

Many grape juice concentrate recipes call for only 6 pints (3.5 litres) of water initially, with sugar to be added later in two stages, within a certain number of days or when a certain S.G. is reached. If you do not want to bother with a hydrometer follow the recipe and you should finish up with a dry wine of between 10% and 12% alcohol, which is the usual range for a table wine.

Why work with a hydrometer?

Adding the sugar in stages and using a hydrometer has the following advantages:
1 You can calculate the sugar content of the must before adding any sugar.
2 You can calculate more accurately the amount of sugar to be added so controlling the final outcome.
3 If there is too much sugar the yeast is apparently overwhelmed and will not become active. By adding sugar in stages, fermentation is more likely to be complete.
4 You can check the progress of fermentation

and stop adding sugar if yeast activity stops.
5 You can calculate the potential alcohol content at the commencement of fermentation and the actual content at the end of the process. The section on the hydrometer has a table at the end which gives the sugar requirements for the must of a dry, medium and sweet wine and also the final sugar content (S.G.) of the finished wine.

Calculating the sugar needed

Having made a gallon of must, measure its S.G. before adding any sugar. Let us say it is 1.050. Then decide upon the alcohol content that you require; 12% is a good target figure. (It is not advisable to try to increase the alcohol content above this figure or the result may just be a sweeter wine. The aim in winemaking is to make a pleasant beverage.
Refer to the S.G. table and it will be seen that 12% alcohol requires 2lb 1oz (938 g) sugar and that a S.G. of 1.050 represents 1lb 1oz (468 g) of sugar, leaving 16oz (450g) to be added.
These figures are for a dry wine, and will need to be adjusted for sweeter results.

Starting fermentation

This sugar should not be added all at once; indeed, if the S.G. reading is over 1.080 and your aim is a dry wine no more should be added at this stage. For a medium wine you could start at 1.085 and for a sweeter one at 1.090. However, remember the total quantity required as it will be added later when the S.G. has dropped.
Leave space for the sugar to be added in the fermentation vessel, 16oz (450g) of sugar needs a pint of water in which to dissolve easily so it is best not to fill a gallon (4.5 litre) container with more than 6 pints (say 3.5 litres) of must initially. Any topping up can be done with must put aside in a sealed container (preferably refrigerated) or with water.

Adding more sugar

The yeast starts off with considerable bubbling and frothing which slows down after four to five days. After about ten days the S.G. should stand at around 1.010.
An addition of half the sugar, dissolved in a small quantity of hot water, can now be made. Fermentation activity will recommence, but not to such a great extent as before.
After a further five days the hydrometer should read about 1.002 and this is the time to add the final quantity of sugar, in syrup form as before.
From now on fermentation will gradually decrease and after four or five weeks the line of bubbles around the top of the container will have died away completely — if not, wait another few days to make sure that no gas is being given off. The hydrometer should now read .990 (in the example given above), up to 1.001 for a medium wine and up to 1.005 for a sweet wine.

Medium to sweet wines

If the wine needs to be sweeter for your taste, you can add more sugar now.
In case fermentation should restart with the addition of this sugar wait a few days to make sure it has completely stopped before racking and sealing.

Actual alcohol present

For an approximate calculation of the actual alcohol content of your finished wine here is a simple formula.
Subtract the S.G. of the wine when fermentation ends (say.990) from the original total S.G. calculation (1.090, for a day wine with 12% alcohol) disregard the decimal point and divide by 8.2.

$$1090 - 990 = \frac{100}{8.2} = 12.2\% \text{ alcohol.}$$

Wine 13 Storing decanting & serving

Storing

Wine is best stored in a cool, well ventilated, dark, dry place with a temperature of 45° to 50°F (7° to 10°C). If straight-sided corks are used and the bottles are stored for longer than two to three weeks, the bottles must be kept on their sides so that the cork remains wet and swelled to maintain a seal. You will also need a rack or racks in which to stack the bottles. Plastic stoppered bottles can be stood upright. Remember, keep the red wines in brown or green bottles and sparkling wines in champagne bottles.

The period before the wine is ready to drink varies widely and can be between six to eight weeks for the concentrates, six to nine months or longer for the fruit and vegetable wines, and even longer — one to two years — for honey based wines such as mead and melomel. However, some 'instant wines' — for which special recipes are given — can be ready within a few weeks of starting.

The period taken from the commencement of storage until the wine is ready for drinking varies according to the main ingredients, the yeast, the temperature and other factors. There is no doubt, however, that as soon as a wine has stopped fermenting it may not taste very pleasant. But as it stands it will gradually become smoother and more mellow.

Wine bottles stacked on their sides for maturing.

FOOD FROM FRANCE

The only sure way to find out if a wine is ready is to taste it, but remember that all wines (except the 'instant' ones) improve with keeping.

Bulk storage and casks

If your wine is stored in a large container the container should be emptied within a week of opening otherwise the wine may turn sour. If you store wine in a wooden cask note that wine drawn off must be replaced reasonably soon or else part of the cask will dry out, also the wine may turn sour.

Any cask not in use should always be stored filled with a sodium metabisulphite solution to prevent the cask from drying out.

Decanting and serving

When the wine is taken from store note if it has any sediment; there is usually a little. If so it should be decanted. Decanting means to pour off the clear wine without disturbing the sediment — this is not difficult if the bottle is emptied at one steady pouring and is not tipped too high, thus avoiding 'glugging' as it pours. The wine can be served from a clean bottle or poured into a jug.

White and rosé wines are normally served chilled. This does not mean refrigerated for several hours! If the wine is too cold the bouquet is lost. Red wines are served at room temperature.

Wine 14 Trouble-shooting faults & remedies

FAULT	CAUSE	REMEDY
Must will not ferment	Too cold	Raise temperature to at least 70°F (21°C).
	Excess of sugar	If a hydrometer reading of must is above 1.090, halve the must and top up each half with water. Start again as if with a fresh must.
	Yeast added too soon after Campden tablets or depectinizer	If Campden tablets or depectinizes are added to a must, 24 hours should elapse before adding yeast. Wait, then add more yeast.
Fermentation stops too soon, and wine too sweet	Too cold or	Raise temperature.
	Yeast action inhibited by high alcohol content or	Try mixing fresh yeast in a starter bottle. Add this to one pint (568 ml) of the wine. When fermentation restarts, add the rest of the wine, one pint (568 ml) at a time, waiting for fermentation to continue before adding the next quantity. If this fails, use the wine for Sangria, wine cups etc, or blend with a very dry wine.
	Yeast action inhibited by too much initial sugar. Lack of yeast nutrient or acid	Try as above, adding yeast nutrient and acid. Alternatively double the quantity of water and start again.

~~REMEDY~~ FAULT	CAUSE	~~FAULT~~ REMEDY
Yeast flavour	Probably use of excessive yeast	Leave in storage for two or three more months—it will slowly cure itself.
Other 'off' flavours	Too long between racking leaving lees in wine	Rack when fermentation is finished and thereafter every eight weeks or as sediment forms.
Wine turns into vinegar	Vinegar fly or bacteria has got into wine	None—discard it. Use sound fruit. Always keep the fermentation vessel covered during the aerobic fermentation period and sealed with an airlock while fermenting. Try adding Campden tablets with the must and for storage.
Fermentation restarts, or will not stop	Yeast not worked out	Add Campden tablets to inhibit yeast action. White wines are prone to restarting fermentation in hot weather.
Crystal formation	Tartaric acid reacting with potassium salts	Refrigerate the wine and rack into a clean container, leaving crystals behind.
Wine is hazy	Pectin haze, pectin destroying enzyme not used	For fruit high in pectin a pectin destroying enzyme should be added before fermentation.
	Starch haze caused by unripe fruit or cereal	These hazes are not always completely removable, but filtering or fining usually cleans them. Always use a cereal yeast for cereal wines.
	Suspended particles in the wine	In general suspended particles can be filtered out.
Insipid wine	Insufficient acid or tannin	Blend with a stronger wine, especially one that is too harsh or acid.
Oiliness or ropiness	The work of lactic acid bacteria	Wine takes on appearance of egg white and goes thick. Beat up wine into a froth and add two Campden tablets per gallon, the taste is not affected.
Moulds	The work of micro-organisms	Caused sometimes when fermentation is slow in starting or utensils not properly sterilized. Skim off mould and add a Campden tablet. After 24 hours add more yeast.

All these faults can be avoided by sterilization, the proper adjustment of additives, the use of Campden tablets to suppress undesirable bacteria and wild yeasts, and the addition of a wine yeast starter in a vigorously fermenting condition.

Wine 15 Recipes A to Z

The recipes that follow have been chosen mainly on the grounds of practicality and availability of the ingredients, but they also afford an opportunity to try some of the more unusual wines.

These recipes must not be considered as hard and fast rules; if the recipe calls for 3½lb (1.59 kg) of sugar and you find that 3lb (1.36 kg) suits your taste better, then use 3lb (1.36 kg). Similarly, if you dislike astringency in wines, do not add any tannin. If they are too acid, cut down the citric acid or lemon juice.

The quantities given all assume that 1 gallon (4.5 litres) of wine is being made; if you want to make 2 or 5 gallons (9 or 23 litres) then just double everything or multiply everything by 5, respectively. If the must is short of the quantity required to fill the fermentation jar, make it up with warm water.

Sugar and the hydrometer

The type of wine (dry, medium or sweet) that you should obtain by exactly following the recipe is stated. If you wish to vary the sweetness (or dryness), it is best to use a hydrometer and add enough sugar, initially, to give an S.G. of 1.080 for a dry wine, 1.085 for a medium one and 1.090 for a sweeter one, following the instructions given elsewhere in this book.

Quantities

Flower petals and leaves are measured by liquid measure, using the gallon or pint markings on a container. The measures given in the recipe assume the petals or leaves to be lightly pressed down.

Washing

In these days of selective weedkillers and garden sprays, some of which are poisonous to man, always wash fruit, leaves and plants thoroughly before starting to make the wine. However, do not wash fruit until you are ready to start making the must as washed fruit deteriorates very rapidly in hot weather.

Temperature

The temperature during the aerobic fermentation period (when fermentation is occurring while the pail is covered with a cloth) should be about 70°F (21°C).

During the anaerobic fermentation period (when the fermentation vessel is sealed with an airlock) the temperature should be about 65°F (18°C).

Almond & raisin wine

Classification: Dessert, Sweet, White

INGREDIENTS	UK/US	METRIC
Almonds	2oz	57g
Raisins	1lb	454g
Lemons, 3		
Sugar, light brown	3lb	1.36kg
Tannin,		
2 to 3 drops or	$\frac{1}{16}$oz	1.75g
Yeast, all-purpose		
Yeast nutrient		
Campden tablets		

1 Blanch (skin) the almonds by soaking in very hot water for a few minutes.
2 Pare the zest from the lemons and squeeze out the juice.
3 Chop the almonds and raisins, deseeding if necessary. Simmer in 1 gallon (4.5 litres) of water for one hour.
4 Strain into a pail and make up the liquid

to 1 gallon (4.5 litres).

5 Add the sugar and stir until dissolved; then add the lemon zest and juice, the tannin, yeast and the yeast nutrient.

6 Cover the pail and stand it in a warm place for 14 days, stirring daily.

7 At the end of this period, strain into a fermentation vessel and insert an airlock.

8 When fermentation is complete, rack the wine into a clean container, add one crushed Campden tablet and close with a bung or safety lock.

9 Rack every two months till clear.

Apple & bilberry wine

Classification: Dessert, Sweet, Red

INGREDIENTS	UK/US	METRIC
Apples, ripe	6lb	2.7kg
Bilberries	4lb	1.8kg
Raisins	8oz	227g
Sugar	3½lb	1.59kg
Citric acid	¼oz	7g
Yeast, all-purpose		
Yeast nutrient		
Campden tablets		
Pectin destroying enzyme		

1 Inspect the apples, cut out any bruised parts and remove the pips.

2 Put them in a pail with ½ gallon (2.3 litres) of cold water and two crushed Campden tablets; stir together.

3 Stir and mash the apples each day for a week, then strain.

4 Three days after preparing the apples, put the bilberries into a second pail and cover

with ½ gallon (2.3 litres) of hot water. Leave for three days, then add the pectin destroying enzyme.

5 After a further 24 hours, thoroughly squeeze out the must and strain it.

6 Mix the two fruit juices together in a third pail, chop up and add the raisins (deseeding if necessary) and add the sugar, citric acid, yeast and yeast nutrient.

7 Stir until the sugar has dissolved, then cover the pail and stand it in a warm place, stirring daily.

8 After two to three weeks, strain into a fermentation vessel and fit an airlock.

9 When fermentation is complete, rack off into a clean container, add one crushed Campden tablet and close with a bung or safety lock.

10 Rack every two months till clear.

Apricot (canned) wine

Classification: Table, Medium, White

1 Proceed exactly as for Peach (canned) Wine, substituting 2lb (907kg) canned apricot halves or pulp for the peaches.

Apricot (dried) wine

Classification: Dessert, Sweet, Golden

INGREDIENTS	UK/US	METRIC
Dried apricots	1lb	454g
Raisins	1lb	454g
Sugar, light brown	3lb	1.36kg
Citric acid	¼oz	7g

	UK/US	METRIC
Tannin, 2 to 3 drops or	$\frac{1}{16}$oz	1.75g
Yeast, all-purpose		
Yeast nutrient		
Campden tablets		
Pectin destroying enzyme		

1 Wash the apricots, cut them up and soak them for 12 hours in enough cold water to cover the fruit.
2 Chop the raisins and deseed if necessary. Place them, with the apricots and the water in which they have soaked, into a pail.
3 Dissolve the sugar in a little hot water and add this to the pail, together with the pectin destroying enzyme.
4 Add the tannin and citric acid and stir thoroughly, then add enough hot water to make up to 1 gallon (4.5 litres).
5 After 24 hours, add the yeast and yeast nutrient.
6 Cover the pail and stand it in a warm place.
7 Leave to ferment for eight days, stirring daily.
8 Strain the must into a fermentation vessel and seal with an airlock.
9 When fermentation is complete, rack into a clean container, add one crushed Campden tablet and close with a bung or safety lock.
10 Rack every two months till clear.

Comment
This wine is an excellent basis for Apricot liqueur.

Apricot (fresh) wine

Classification: Table, Medium, Golden

INGREDIENTS	UK/US	METRIC
Apricots, ripe and sweet	4lb	1.8kg
Sugar	3lb	1.36kg
Citric acid	$\frac{1}{4}$oz	7g
Tannin, 2 or 3 drops or	$\frac{1}{16}$oz	1.75g
Yeast, all-purpose		
Yeast nutrient		
Campden tablets		
Pectin destroying enzyme		

1 Wash the apricots well and allow them to drain.
2 Put the apricots into a pan and boil with 1¼ gallons (5.7 litres) of water.
3 Take out the stones, crack 12 stones and remove the kernels. Add the kernels to the pan and boil for another 10 minutes.
4 Strain the liquid into a pail; add the sugar, citric acid, tannin and pectin destroying enzyme. Stir well until the sugar has dissolved, leave for 24 hours.
5 Add the yeast and nutrient, cover the pail and stand it in a warm place. Stir daily.
6 After three days, strain the must into a fermentation jar and seal it with an airlock.
7 When fermentation is complete, rack the wine into a container, add one crushed Campden tablet, and close with a bung or safety lock.
8 Rack every two months, for six months, then less frequently as sediment forms.

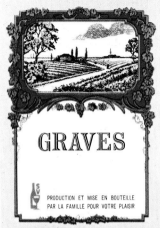

GRAVES

PRODUCTION ET MISE EN BOUTEILLE
PAR LA FAMILLE POUR VOTRE PLAISIR

BURGUNDY

PRODUCTION ET MISE EN BOUTEILLE PAR LA FAMILLE POUR VOTRE PLAISIR

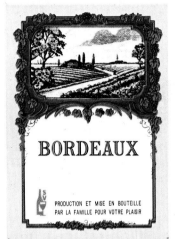

BORDEAUX

PRODUCTION ET MISE EN BOUTEILLE
PAR LA FAMILLE POUR VOTRE PLAISIR

CHABLIS

PRODUCTION ET MISE EN BOUTEILLE
PAR LA FAMILLE POUR VOTRE PLAISIR

Riesling

PRODUZIERT UND ABGEFÜLLT VON
DER FAMILIE FÜR IHREN GENUSS

VIN ROSÉ

MARQUE   DÉPOSÉE

PRODUCTION ET MISE EN BOUTEILLE
PAR LA FAMILLE POUR VOTRE PLAISIR

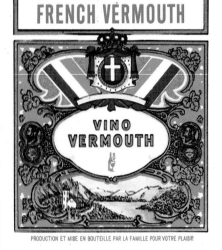

FRENCH VERMOUTH

VINO
VERMOUTH

PRODUCTION ET MISE EN BOUTEILLE PAR LA FAMILLE POUR VOTRE PLAISIR

VARIETY OF WINE Banana

Amount made 1 Gallons   Wine begun on 7 June 1962

INGREDIENTS

4 lb bananas
4 oz raisins
1 orange, 1 lemon

Specific Gravity of Must alone :—

Water 1 Gallons   Yeast Variety all purpose
                     Yeast Nutrient (nutrient)

Sugar 4 lb 1st addition .... lbs. on ....

        2nd addition .... lbs. on ....

        3rd addition .... lbs. on ....

Other Ingredients ½ oz citric acid; ⅓ oz tannin

Specific Gravity with Sugar etc. 1.155

Wine yeasted on 7.6.62   Fermentation begins on 8.6.62

Dates of Rackings	Specific Gravity	Additions	Remarks
1st on 15 July			
2nd on 18 Sept			
3rd on March '63			
4th on			
5th on			
6th on			

Wine finally bottled on 18 March 1963

Specific Gravity 1.003   Alcohol content ....

Type of Wine White, sweet   Bin No. 43

64

Banana wine

Classification: Dessert, Sweet, White

INGREDIENTS	UK/US	METRIC
Bananas, old and very ripe	4lb	1.8kg
Raisins	4oz	113g
Orange, 1		
Lemon, 1		
Sugar	3lb	1.36kg
Citric acid	½oz	14g
Tannin, 4 to 6 drops or	⅛oz	3.5g
Yeast, all-purpose		
Yeast nutrient		
Campden tablets		

1 Peel the bananas, retaining about ½lb (227g) of their skins.
2 Put the bananas and skins in a muslin (or cheesecloth) bag, place it in a large pan or boiler with 1¼ gallons (5.7 litres) of water and simmer for half hour.
3 Squeeze the juice from the orange and lemon.
4 Place the sugar, orange and lemon juice, chopped deseeded raisins, tannin and citric acid in a pail.
5 Pour the liquid from the bananas into the pail, and stir until the sugar is fully dissolved.
6 When cool, squeeze as much juice as possible from the bag into the pail.
7 Add the yeast and yeast nutrient.
8 Cover the pail and stand it in a warm place for seven days, stirring daily.
9 Strain off the juice into a fermentation vessel, and close it with an airlock.
10 When fermentation is complete, rack into a clean container, add one crushed Campden tablet and close with a bung or safety lock.
11 Rack every two months till clear.

A selection of labels for homemade wines and a page from a wine log book. Don't forget to write the date of bottling on the label.

65

Barley & raisin wine

Classification: Table, Medium, White

INGREDIENTS	UK/US	METRIC
Whole barley grains	1lb	454g
Raisins	1lb	454g
Potatoes	1lb	454g
Sugar	3½lb	1.59kg
Citric acid	½oz	14g
Tannin,		
2 to 3 drops or	$\frac{1}{16}$oz	1.75g
Yeast, cereal-type		
Yeast nutrient		
Campden tablets		

1 Soak the barley in water overnight.
2 Peel and chop up the potatoes.
3 Deseed the raisins if necessary, mix them with the barley and put the mixture through a mincer or grinder.
4 Put the chopped potatoes, minced barley and raisins, and sugar into a pail.
5 Heat almost to boiling point sufficient water to cover the contents of the pail, and pour it in.
6 Add the citric acid and tannin.
7 Add one crushed Campden tablet, then cover the pail.
8 After 24 hours, add the yeast and nutrient, and place the pail in a warm place to ferment.
9 Leave for 10 days, stirring daily.
10 Strain the liquid into a fermentation vessel, make it up to 1 gallon (4.5 litres) and fit an airlock.
11 When fermentation is complete, rack into a clean container, add one crushed Campden tablet and close the container with a bung or safety lock.
12 Rack every two months till clear.

Comment
An easily made wine, needing no boiling or mashing, which usually clears very quickly.

Barley is often used in winemaking. Here are various forms of available barley: whole grains, flaked and ground barley, Ground barley is used in the Greengage Wine recipe. A cereal yeast is recommended when fermenting barley.

DON LAST

Beetroot (beet) wine

Classification: Table, Medium, Red

INGREDIENTS	UK/US	METRIC
Beetroot (beet)	4lb	1.8kg
Lemon, 1		
Ginger root, 1 piece		
Sugar	3½lb	1.59kg
Citric acid	½oz	14g
Tannin,		
4 to 6 drops or	⅛oz	3.5g
Yeast, all-purpose		
Yeast nutrient		
Campden tablets		

1 Wash the beetroot; do not skin.
2 Slice the beetroot into 1 gallon (4.5 litres) of water and simmer it until the vegetable is tender.
3 Squeeze the juice from the lemon, and 'bruise' the ginger.
4 Strain the liquid from the beetroot into a pail; add the lemon juice, the piece of ginger, the sugar, the citric acid and the tannin; stir until the sugar has dissolved.
5 Add hot water to make the volume up to 1 gallon (4.5 litres), then add the yeast and the nutrient.
6 Cover the pail and stand it in a warm place for three days, stirring daily.
7 Strain off the juice into a fermentation vessel and close it with an airlock.
8 When fermentation is complete, rack into a clean container, add one crushed Campden tablet and close with a bung or safety lock.
9 Rack every two months till clear.

Comment
Keep this wine in the dark as much as possible or the wine will turn brown instead of remaining a bright red.

Bilberry (canned) wine

Classification: Table, Medium dry, Red

INGREDIENTS	UK/US	METRIC
Bilberries	2lb	907g
Sugar	2½lb	1.13kg
Citric acid	¼oz	7g
Yeast, all-purpose		
Yeast nutrient		
Campden tablets		
Pectin destroying enzyme		

1 Proceed as for Peach (canned) Wine except that, as there is tannin already present in bilberries, additional tannin need not be added.

Bilberry & raisin (dried) wine

Classification: Dessert, Sweet, Red

INGREDIENTS	UK/US	METRIC
Dried bilberries	1lb	454g
Raisins	1lb	454g
Lemons, 3		
Sugar	3lb	1.36kg
Yeast, all-purpose		
Yeast nutrient		
Campden tablets		

**Pectin destroying
enzyme**

1 Thoroughly wash the bilberries.
2 Soak them in 2 pints (1.14 litres) of hot
water for 12 hours, keeping the pail covered.
3 Dissolve half of the sugar in 3 pints (1.7
litres) of hot water; when cool, add this to the
bilberries.
4 Chop and deseed the raisins and add these
to the pail, then fill it to 1 gallon (4.5 litres)
with hot water.
5 Pare the zest from the lemons, squeeze the
juice from them and add to the pail, with the
remainder of the sugar and the pectin
destroying enzyme.
6 Stir well until the sugar has dissolved, then,
after 24 hours, add the yeast and nutrient.
7 Cover the pail and stand it in a warm place
for seven days, stirring daily.
8 Strain juice into a fermentation vessel and
seal with an airlock.
9 When fermentation is complete, rack the
must into a clean container, add one crushed
Campden tablet and close it with a bung or
safety lock.
10 Rack every two months till clear.

Bilberry (fresh) wine

Classification: Table, Dry, Red
1 Make as for Blueberry wine, substituting
2lb (907g) bilberries.

Comment
In Scotland, bilberries are called blaeberries,
and another local name is whortle berry.

Birch sap & pear wine

Classification: Table, Medium, White

INGREDIENTS	UK/US	METRIC
Birch sap	6 pints	3.4 litres
Pears, ripe	12 oz	340g
Sultanas (or white raisins)	8oz	227g
Sugar	3lb	1.36kg
Citric acid	$\frac{1}{2}$oz	14g
Tannin, 2 to 3 drops or	$\frac{1}{16}$oz	1.75g
Yeast, all-purpose		
Yeast nutrient		
Campden tablets		

1 Deseed and chop up the sultanas.
2 Peel the pears and cut them into small
pieces, removing the pips.
3 Put the pears into a pan, add a crushed
Campden tablet and water to cover.
Bring to the boil, then simmer for 15 minutes.
Add the sap, bring to the boil and remove
from heat.
4 Put the sultanas into a pail and pour in the
sap and pear mixture.
5 Add the citric acid and tannin and stir well.
6 Dissolve the sugar in a little hot water and
pour this into the pail.
7 Add the yeast and nutrient, stir and cover.
Stand it in a warm place for five days,
stirring daily.
8 Strain into a fermentation vessel, make it
up to 1 gallon (4.5 litres) of must with warm
water and fit an airlock.
9 When fermentation is complete, rack the
wine into a clean container, add one crushed
Campden tablet and close it with a bung or
safety lock.
10 Rack every two months, for six months,
then at longer intervals as sediment forms.

Blackberry wine

Classification: Dessert, Sweet, Red

INGREDIENTS	UK/US	METRIC
Blackberries	4lb	1.8kg
Lemon, 1		
Sugar, light brown	3lb	1.36kg
Citric acid	¼oz	7g
Tannin,		
4 to 6 drops or	⅛oz	3.5g
Yeast, all-purpose*		
Yeast nutrient		
Campden tablets		
Pectin destroying		
enzyme		

1 Wash the berries, and allow them to drain.
2 Soak the berries, with a crushed Campden tablet, in cold water; this will bring out any worms. Remove them! Rinse the fruit and drain.
3 Pare the zest from the lemon, and squeeze out the juice.
4 Put the berries, lemon juice, rind, citric acid and tannin into a pail, and pour 1 gallon (4.5 litres) of boiling water over them, to cover. Crush the fruit with the back of a large spoon.
5 Cover the pail and allow it to stand for two days, stirring daily.
6 Add the pectin destroying enzyme and leave for a further 24 hours.
7 Dissolve the sugar in a little hot water.
8 Strain the juice from the berries into a second pail and add the sugar syrup, yeast and nutrient.
9 Cover the pail and stand it in a warm place for three days, stirring daily.
10 Strain into a fermentation vessel, and fit an airlock.
11 When fermentation is complete, rack into a clean container, add one crushed Campden tablet and seal the fermentation vessel with a bung or safety lock.
12 Rack every two months, till clear.

Comment
*Burgundy-type cultured yeast can be used as an alternative.

Blackcurrant wine

Classification: Dessert, Sweet, Red

INGREDIENTS	UK/US	METRIC
Blackcurrants	4lb	1.8kg
Sugar	3½lb	1.59kg
Citric acid	¼oz	7g
Yeast, all-purpose		
Yeast nutrient		
Campden tablets		
Pectin destroying		
enzyme		

1 Wash the currants carefully and remove the stems.
2 Put the currants and 1 gallon (4.5 litres) of water into a pan and bring to the boil, then simmer for 20 minutes.
3 Strain the liquid into a pail.
4 Add the sugar and stir until the sugar is dissolved.
5 When lukewarm, add the citric acid and pectin destroying enzyme.
6 Cover the pail, then stand it in a warm place.
7 After 24 hours, add the yeast and nutrient.
8 After 14 days, strain the must into a fermentation jar and seal it with an airlock.
9 When fermentation has finished, rack the wine into a clean container, add one crushed Campden tablet and close the container with a bung or safety lock.
10 Rack every two months, for six months, then at longer intervals as sediment forms.

Blueberry wine

Classification: Table, Dry, Red

INGREDIENTS	UK/US	METRIC
Blueberries (fresh)	2lb	907g
Sugar	2lb	907g
Citric acid	¼oz	7g
Yeast, all-purpose		
Yeast nutrient		
Campden tablets		
Pectin destroying enzyme		

1 Wash and drain the berries.
2 Put the berries into a pail and pour ½ gallon (2.3 litres) of boiling water over them.
3 Stir in the sugar and citric acid, then add a further ½ gallon (2.3 litres) of very hot water and stir until the sugar has dissolved.
4 When the must is lukewarm, add the pectin destroying enzyme.
5 After 24 hours, add the yeast and nutrient.
6 Cover the pail and stand it in a warm place for four to five days, stirring daily.
7 Strain the must into a fermentation vessel and close it with an airlock.
8 When fermentation is complete, rack into a clean container, add one crushed Campden tablet and close it with a bung or safety lock.
9 Rack every two months.

Burgundy wine

Classification: Table, Dry, Red

INGREDIENTS	UK/US	METRIC
Burgundy grape juice concentrate, 1 can	2lb 3oz	1kg
Sugar	10oz	284g
Yeast, all-purpose*		
Yeast nutrient		
Campden tablets		

1 Proceed exactly as for Vin Ordinaire. If a really astringent wine is preferred, tannin may be added before fermentation.

Comment
*Burgundy-type cultured yeast could be used if preferred.

Carnation & raisin wine

Classification: Table, Medium, Red

INGREDIENTS	UK/US	METRIC
Carnation flowers, red, scented	½ gallon	2.3 litres
Sultanas (or white raisins)	6oz	170g
Lemon, 1		
Orange, 1		
Sugar	3lb	1.36kg
Citric acid	¼oz	7g
Tannin, 2 to 3 drops or	$\frac{1}{16}$oz	1.75g
Yeast, all-purpose		

Yeast nutrient
Campden tablets

1 Follow the method for Rose Petal Wine, exactly.

Carrot & citrus wine

Classification: Table, Medium, Rosé

INGREDIENTS	UK/US	METRIC
Carrots, large (but not old)	6lb	2.7kg
Oranges, 4		
Lemons, 4		
Raisins	8oz	227g
Sugar, Demerara or light brown	4lb	1.8kg
Tannin, 2 to 3 drops or	$\frac{1}{16}$oz	1.75g
Yeast, all-purpose		
Yeast nutrient		
Campden tablets		
Black pepper, ground	$\frac{1}{4}$oz	7g

1 Thoroughly wash the carrots, but do not peel them, and trim off the ends.
2 Grate the carrots and place them in a pan with 1¼ gallons (5.7 litres) of water.
3 Boil the mixture for 40 minutes.
4 When cool, strain the liquid into a pail, squeezing out as much juice from the carrots as possible.
5 Add the sugar and stir until dissolved.
6 Pare the zest from the citrus fruit and squeeze out the juice.
7 Chop up the raisins and deseed if necessary.
8 Add the citrus zest and juice, the raisins, pepper, tannin, yeast and nutrient; stir well.
9 Cover the pail and stand in a warm place; stir daily.
10 After two weeks, strain the must into a fermentation vessel and seal with an airlock.
11 When fermentation is complete, rack the wine into a clean container, add one crushed Campden tablet and close the container with a bung or a safety lock.
12 Rack every two months, for six months, then less frequently till clear.

Celery wine

Classification: Table, Medium, White

INGREDIENTS	UK/US	METRIC
Celery,	4lb	1.8kg
Sultanas (or white raisins)	8oz	227g
Lemons, 2		
Sugar, light brown	3lb	1.36kg
Tannin, 2 to 3 drops or	$\frac{1}{16}$oz	1.75g
Yeast, all-purpose		
Yeast nutrient		
Citric acid	$\frac{1}{4}$oz	7g
Campden tablets		

1 Wash the celery thoroughly, discarding the leaves, but retaining both the white and green stems.
2 Cut the stems into short lengths, add water to cover and boil until tender.
3 Strain the liquor into a pail, and add the chopped sultanas and citric acid.
4 Make up to 1 gallon (4.5 litres) with hot water; squeeze the juice from the lemons.
5 Add the sugar and lemon juice, and stir until the sugar is fully dissolved.
6 When the must has cooled, add the yeast, nutrient and tannin.
7 Cover the pail and stand it in a warm place, stirring daily.
8 After 12 days, strain the must into a fermentation vessel and seal it with an airlock.
9 When fermentation is complete, rack into a clean container, add one crushed Campden tablet and close with a bung or safety lock.
10 Rack every two months till clear.

Cherry wine

Classification: Dessert, Sweet, Rosé

INGREDIENTS	UK/US	METRIC
Morello cherries, ripe	8lb	3.6kg
Sugar	3½lb	1.5kg
Citric acid	½oz	14g
Tannin, 2 to 3 drops or	$\frac{1}{16}$oz	1.75g
Yeast, all-purpose		
Yeast nutrient		
Campden tablets		
Pectin destroying enzyme		

1 Wash the fruit thoroughly and allow it to drain.
2 Place the fruit in a large pail and cover it with 1 gallon (4.5 litres) of cold water.
3 Add one crushed Campden tablet, the citric acid and tannin. Cover the pail with a cloth and allow it to stand for five days, gradually crushing the cherries.
4 Dissolve the sugar in a little hot water and add this to the pail, stirring well, then add the pectin destroying enzyme.
5 After a further five days, add the yeast and nutrient, cover the pail and stand it in a warm place, stirring daily.
6 After four more days, strain the must into a fermentation vessel and seal it with an airlock.
7 When fermentation is complete, rack the wine into a clean container, add one crushed Campden tablet and close it with a bung or safety lock.
8 Rack every two month till clear.

NELSON HARGREAVES

Clover & citrus wine

Classification: Table, Medium, White

INGREDIENTS	UK/US	METRIC
Pink clover flowers	½ gallon	2.3 litres
Lemons 2		
Oranges, 2		
Ginger root, 1 piece		
Sugar	3lb	1.36kg
Citric acid	½oz	14g
Tannin,		
2 to 3 drops or	$\frac{1}{16}$oz	1.75g
Yeast, all-purpose		
Yeast nutrient		
Campden tablets		
Pectin destroying enzyme		

1 Wash the flowers.
2 Pare the zest and squeeze the juice from the oranges and lemons. 'Bruise' the ginger.
3 Put the flowers, sugar, orange and lemon juice and zest, bruised ginger, citric acid and tannin, with 1 gallon (4.5 litres) of water, into a pan.
4 Bring the fluid to the boil and simmer for 30 minutes, stirring frequently, then strain it into a pail.
5 When the liquid is lukewarm, add the pectin destroying enzyme and cover the pail.
6 After 24 hours, add the yeast and nutrient, then stand the pail in a warm place for 14 days, stirring daily.
7 At the end of this period, strain into a fermentation vessel, and insert an airlock.
8 When fermentation is complete, rack the wine into a clean container, add one crushed Campden tablet and close it with a bung or safety lock.
9 Rack every two months till clear.

Sweet Cherry Wine is an excellent alternative for Madeira or Port at the end of a meal.

Cornmeal wine

Classification: Table, Medium, White

INGREDIENTS	UK/US	METRIC
Cornmeal	1lb	454g
Lemons, 2		
Oranges, 2		
Grape juice sweet concentrate (white), ½ can	1lb 1½oz	492g
Sugar	1½lb	680g
Citric acid	½oz	14g
Yeast, all-purpose		
Yeast nutrient		
Campden tablets		

1 Squeeze the juice from the citus fruit.
2 Add this juice, the grape juice concentrate, the citric acid, sugar and cornmeal to a pail. Add ¾ gallon (3.4 litres) of very hot water and stir thoroughly until the sugar has dissolved.
3 Pour the complete contents of the pail into a fermentation vessel, add warm water to make up to 1 gallon (4.5 litres) then the yeast and nutrient; fit an airlock.
4 Stand the vessel in a warm place until fermentation ceases.
5 Rack into a clean container, add one crushed Campden tablet and close the container with a bung or safety lock.
6 Rack after four weeks, and before bottling.

Cyser

Classification: Table, Medium, White

INGREDIENTS	UK/US	METRIC
Dessert apples	1½lb	608g
Crab apples	1½lb	680g
Honey	3lb	1.36kg

Citric acid	$\frac{1}{4}$oz	7g
Tannin,		
2 to 3 drops or	$\frac{1}{16}$oz	1.75g
Yeast, all-purpose		
Yeast nutrient		
Campden tablets		

1 Wash the apples, cut out any bruised parts and remove the pips.
2 Mince the apples, then squeeze and strain the juice into a pail.
3 Add two crushed Campden tablets and stir these in.
4 Dissolve the honey in hot water and simmer for 5 minutes then add it to the pail, with the citric acid and tannin. Allow it to stand for 24 hours.
5 Make up to 1 gallon (4.5 litres) with hot water, then add the yeast and nutrient.
6 Cover the pail and stand it in a warm place, stirring daily.
7 After seven days, strain the juice into a fermentation vessel and fit an airlock.
8 When fermentation is complete, rack the wine into a clean container, add one crushed Campden tablet and close the container with a bung or safety lock.
9 Rack every two months, for six months, then less frequently as sediment forms.

1 Wash the fruit gently, and drain it.
2 Put the fruit in a pail and pour over it $\frac{1}{4}$ gallon (1.14 litres) of boiling water.
3 Add 1lb (454g) of the sugar and citric acid. Stir until the sugar has dissolved and break up the fruit with a large spoon.
4 Add a further $\frac{1}{2}$ gallon (2.3 litres) of warm water, then add the pectin destroying enzyme; cover the pail and stand it in a warm place, stirring daily.
5 After two days, strain it into a fermentation vessel, then dissolve 1$\frac{1}{2}$lb (454g) of sugar in hot water and add this to the vessel.
6 Add the yeast and nutrient, then make up to 1 gallon (4.5 litres) with warm water and seal the vessel with an airlock.
7 When fermentation is complete, rack into a clean container, add one crushed Campden tablet and close the container with a bung or safety lock.
8 Rack every two months till clear.

Damson plum wine

Classification: Table, Dry, Red

INGREDIENTS	UK/US	METRIC
Damson plums	3lb	1.36kg
Sugar	2$\frac{1}{2}$lb	1.13kg
Citric acid	$\frac{1}{4}$oz	7g
Yeast, all-purpose		
Yeast nutrient		
Campden tablets		
Pectin destroying enzyme		

Dandelion wine

Classification: Table, Medium, White

INGREDIENTS	UK/US	METRIC
Dandelion flowers	$\frac{3}{4}$ gallon	3.4 litres
Lemon, 1		
Orange, 1		
Ginger root, 1 piece		
Sugar	3lb	1.36kg
Citric acid	$\frac{1}{4}$oz	7g
Tannin,		
2 to 3 drops or	$\frac{1}{16}$oz	1.75g

Yeast, all-purpose
Yeast nutrient
Campden tablets
Pectin destroying
enzyme

1 Wash the flowers thoroughly and drain them.
2 Put the flowers in a pail and cover them with 1 gallon (4.5 litres) of boiling water.
3 Cover the pail and leave it for three days, stirring daily.
4 Pare the zest from the citrus fruit and squeeze out the juice; 'bruise' the ginger root.
5 Thoroughly squeeze out the flowers into a pan, then add the citrus zest and juice, ginger root, citric acid, tannin and sugar. Stir well to dissolve the sugar while bringing to the boil.
6 Boil for 30 minutes, then pour into a pail.
7 When cool, add the pectin destroying enzyme; cover the container and stand it in a warm place.
8 After 24 hours, add the yeast and yeast nutrient. Stir daily.
9 After six days, strain the liquor into a fermentation vessel and seal it.
10 When fermentation is complete, rack the wine into a clean container, add one crushed Campden tablet and close it with a bung or safety lock.
11 Rack every two months, for six months, then rack again as the sediment settles.

Elderberry punch

Classification: For winter nights

INGREDIENTS	UK/US	METRIC
Elderberry wine, 2 bottles		
Brandy	4fl oz	114ml
Oranges, 4		
Lemons, 2		
Cloves	$\frac{1}{4}$oz	7g
Sugar (to taste)		
Cinnamon stick	$\frac{1}{2}$ oz	14g

1 Pare the zest from the oranges and lemons, and squeeze out the juice. Put the cloves and cinnamon in a muslin or cheesecloth bag.
2 Put the zest and the juice into a jug, together with the bag of spices and the wine.
3 Stand the jug in a warm place for two hours, then strain the punch into a pan.
4 Heat, but do not overheat, or the alcohol will evaporate.
5 Add the brandy and serve hot, with sugar added to taste.

Elderberry wine

Classification: Dessert, Sweet, Red

INGREDIENTS	UK/US	METRIC
Ripe elderberries	4lb	1.8kg
Raisins	8oz	227g
Ginger root, 1 piece		
Lemon, 1		
Sugar	3lb	1.36kg
Citric acid	$\frac{1}{4}$oz	7g
Yeast, all-purpose		
Yeast nutrient		
Campden tablets		

Pectin destroying enzyme

1 Wash the sprays of berries thoroughly, then strip the berries from their stalks.
2 Boil the berries in 1 gallon (4.5 litres) of water, for 10 minutes.
3 Squeeze the juice from the lemon, chop and deseed the raisins and 'bruise' the ginger.
4 Strain the juice from the berries and return the juice to the pan.
5 Add the raisins, sugar, lemon juice, citric acid and bruised ginger, then simmer together for 20 minutes.
6 When the mixture is cool, transfer it to a pail and add the pectin destroying enzyme; cover the pail.
7 After 24 hours, add the yeast and nutrient.
8 Stand the pail in a warm place for three weeks, stirring daily.
9 At the end of this period, strain the juice into a fermentation vessel and fit an airlock.
10 When fermentation is complete, rack into a clean container with one crushed Campden tablet, and close the container with a bung or safety lock.
11 Rack every two months till clear before bottling.

Gluwein is a good warming drink in cold weather.

Gluwein

Classification: For the winter nights

INGREDIENTS	UK/US	METRIC
Red wine, 1 bottle		
Mulling spices, 1 packet		
Sugar	2oz	57g

1 Tie the spices in a muslin or cheesecloth bag, then put them in a pan with the wine and sugar.
2 Heat the wine, but do not overheat, or the alcohol will evaporate. Taste occasionally removing the spices when their flavour is sufficiently strong.

Gooseberry (green) wine

Classification: Table, Dry, White

INGREDIENTS	UK/US	METRIC
Gooseberries, green and ripe	4lb	1.8kg
Sugar	2½lb	1.13kg
Citric acid	¼oz	7g
Tannin, 2 to 3 drops or	$\frac{1}{16}$oz	1.75g
Yeast, all-purpose		
Yeast nutrient		
Campden tablets		
Pectin destroying enzyme		

1 'Top and tail' and wash the gooseberries.
2 Put the gooseberries in a pail and add ½ gallon (2.3 litres) of hot water.
3 Cover and stand the pail for three days, mashing daily.
4 Dissolve the sugar in some hot water.
5 Strain the liquid from the gooseberries and add, with the sugar syrup, the tannin, citric acid and pectin destroying enzyme, to the fermentation vessel, stir thoroughly.
6 After 24 hours add the yeast and nutrient, make up to 1 gallon (4.5 litres) of water and seal the vessel with an airlock.
7 When fermentation is complete, rack the wine into a clean container, add one crushed Campden tablet and close the container with a bung or safety lock.
8 Rack every two months till clear.

Grapefruit juice wine

Classification: Dessert, Sweet, White

INGREDIENTS	UK/US	METRIC
Grapefruit juice, 1 can (sweetened)*	1lb 3oz	538g
Orange, 1		
Lemon, 1		
Sugar	2½lb	1.13kg
Tannin, 2 to 3 drops or	1/16 oz	1.75g
Yeast, all-purpose		
Yeast nutrient		
Campden tablets		
Pectin destroying enzyme		

1 Pare the zest from the orange and lemon, and squeeze out the juice.
2 Dissolve the sugar in hot water and pour it into the fermentation vessel.
3 Add the citrus zest and juice, and grapefruit juice.

4 Add the tannin and pectin destroying enzyme, with ½ gallon (2.3 litres) of warm water.
5 After 24 hours, add the yeast and yeast nutrient; make up to 1 gallon (4.5 litres).
6 Seal the vessel with an airlock, and stand it in a warm place.
7 When fermentation is complete, rack the wine into a clean container, add one crushed Campden tablet and seal it with a bung or safety lock.
8 Rack after three weeks, and again before bottling.

Comment
*If unsweetened juice is used, add 3lb (1.36kg) of sugar.

Greengage wine

Classification: Table, Medium, White

INGREDIENTS	UK/US	METRIC
Greengage plums, ripe	3lb	1.36kg
Ground barley	6oz	170g
Sugar	3lb	1.36kg

Citric acid	$\frac{1}{4}$oz	7g
Tannin,		
2 to 3 drops or	$\frac{1}{16}$oz	1.75g
Yeast, cereal-type		
Yeast nutrient		
Campden tablets		
Pectin destroying		
enzyme		

1 Rinse the fruit gently, and allow it to drain.
2 Put the fruit in a pail with the barley and pour 1 gallon (4.5 litres) of boiling water into the pail. Cover it and leave for four days.
3 At the end of this period, strain the liquid into a second pail, and add the sugar, citric acid, tannin and pectin destroying enzyme. Stir well to dissolve the sugar, and cover the pail.
4 After 24 hours, add the yeast and nutrient, stir again, and stand the pail in a warm place. Stir daily.
5 After seven days, strain the must into a fermentation vessel and seal it with an airlock.
6 When fermentation is complete, rack the wine into a container, add one crushed Campden tablet and close it with a bung or safety lock.
7 Rack every two months till clear.

Hock wine

Classification: Table, Dry, White

INGREDIENTS	UK/US	METRIC
Hock grape juice concentrate, 1 can	2lb 3oz	1kg
Sugar	10oz	284g
Yeast, all-purpose*		
Yeast nutrient		
Campden tablets		

1 Proceed exactly as for Vin Ordinaire.

Comment
*Hock-Type cultured yeast could be used if preferred.

Honeysuckle wine

Classification: Table, Medium, White

INGREDIENTS	UK/US	METRIC
Honeysuckle blossom	2 pints	1.14 litres
Raisins	4oz	113g
Lemon, 1		
Orange, 1		
Sugar	3lb	1.36kg
Citric acid	$\frac{1}{4}$oz	7g
Tannin,		
2 to 3 drops or	$\frac{1}{16}$oz	1.75g
Yeast, all-purpose		
Yeast nutrient		
Campden tablets		

1 Wash the flowers gently and drain them.
2 Deseed and chop the raisins, pare the zest from the citrus fruit and squeeze the juice from it.
3 Place the flowers, raisins, zest and juice from the fruit in a pail and add a crushed Campden tablet.
4 Add 1 gallon (4.5 litres) of hot water to the pail, stir well, cover it and leave for 24 hours.
5 Dissolve the sugar in hot water and add this to the must with the citric acid and tannin.

6 Add the yeast and nutrient, stir well, cover the pail and stand it in a warm place.
7 After seven days, strain the must into a fermentation vessel and seal it.
8 When fermentation has ceased, rack the wine into a clean container, add one crushed Campden tablet and close it with a bung or safety lock.
9 Rack every two months till clear.

Loganberry wine

Classification: Table, Medium, Rosé

INGREDIENTS	UK/US	METRIC
Loganberries	4lb	1.8kg
Sugar, light brown	3lb	1.36kg
Citric acid	$\frac{1}{4}$oz	7g
Yeast, all-purpose		
Yeast nutrient		
Campden tablets		
Pectin destroying enzyme		

1 Follow the same method as for Blackberry Wine, omitting the lemon and tannin.

Marigold wine

Classification: Table, Medium, White

INGREDIENTS	UK/US	METRIC
Marigold flowers (heads)	$\frac{3}{4}$ gallon	3.4 litres
Lemons, 2		
Sugar	3lb	1.36kg
Tannin, 2 to 3 drops or	$\frac{1}{16}$oz	1.75g
Yeast, all-purpose		
Yeast nutrient		
Campden tablets		

1 Thoroughly wash the flowers, and drain them.
2 Dissolve the sugar in a little hot water.
3 Pare the zest from the lemons and squeeze out the juice.
4 Put the flowers, sugar, tannin, lemon zest and juice into a pail and make up to 1 gallon (4.5 litres) with hot water.
5 When the mixture has cooled, add the yeast and nutrient.
6 Cover the pail and stand it in a warm place, stirring daily.
7 After seven days, strain the must into a fermentation vessel and close it with an airlock.
8 When fermentation is complete, rack into a clean container, add one crushed Campden tablet and close the container with a bung or safety lock.
9 Rack every two months till clear.

Mead

Classification: Table, Dry, White

INGREDIENTS	UK/US	METRIC
Honey (light)	3lb	1.36kg
Orange, 1		
Lemon, 1		
Sugar cubes – 1 per bottle		
Citric acid	$\frac{1}{2}$oz	14g
Tannin, 2 to 3 drops or	$\frac{1}{16}$oz	1.75g
Yeast, all-purpose		

Yeast nutrient
Campden tablets

1 Put the honey into a pan and add hot water to make up to 1 gallon (4.5 litres).
2 Stir well over heat until the honey has melted, then retain a low heat for a further five minutes.
3 Squeeze the lemon and orange, retaining the juice.
4 Add to the melted honey the lemon and orange juice, the tannin, citric acid, the yeast and the nutrient.
5 Strain the liquid into a fermentation vessel, stand it in a warm place and plug the vessel with cotton wool (absorbent cotton).
6 After four days, fit a fermentation lock.
7 When fermentation is complete, rack into a clean container, add one crushed Campden tablet and close the container with a bung or safety lock.
8 When cleared, rack into strong bottles (screw top beer bottles or champagne bottles), add a cube of sugar to each bottle and close them. Tie down the corks or stoppers.

Melomel

Classification: Dessert, Sweet, Red

INGREDIENTS	UK/US	METRIC
Blackcurrants	3lb	1.36kg
Honey, light	4lb	1.8kg
Lemons, 2		
Yeast, all-purpose		
Yeast nutrient		
Campden tablets		
Pectin destroying enzyme ·		

1 Strip the blackcurrants from their stalks, then wash and drain them.
2 Pare the zest from the lemons and squeeze out the juice.
3 Put the currants into a pail, crush them, add the pectin destroying enzyme, the zest

and juice of the lemons and one crushed Campden tablet.
4 Add 6 pints (3.4 litres) of cold water to the pail, stir well, cover it and leave it for 24 hours.
5 Dissolve the honey in a little hot water and simmer for five minutes. Add this to the pail.
6 Stir in the yeast and yeast nutrient, cover the pail and stand it in a warm place for two days, stirring daily.
7 Strain the must into a fermentation vessel, add water to make 1 gallon (4.5 litres) and seal the vessel with an airlock.
8 When fermentation is complete, rack the wine into a clean container, add one crushed Campden tablet and close the container with a bung or safety lock.
9 Rack every two months, for six months, then less frequently as sediment forms.

Comment
Any fruit, except apples, can be mixed with the honey to make melomel. A less strongly flavoured fruit such as rose hips, with 1lb (454g) less honey, will make a dry melomel.

Mixed dried fruit wine

Classification: Dessert, Sweet, White

INGREDIENTS	UK/US	METRIC
Raisins	4oz	113g
Currants	4oz	113g
Sultanas (or white raisins)	2 oz	57g
Candied peel	2oz	57g
Whole wheat grains	1lb	454g
Sugar	3lb	1.36kg
Citric acid	$\frac{1}{2}$oz	14g
Tannin, 2 to 3 drops or	$\frac{1}{16}$oz	1.75g
Yeast, cereal-type		
Yeast nutrient		
Campden tablets		

Pectin destroying enzyme

1 Wash and chop up the currants, sultanas and raisins, deseeding if necessary.
2 Put this dried fruit with the candied peel, sugar and wheat in a pail.
3 Pour 1 gallon (4.5 litres) boiling water into the pail and stir well until all the sugar has dissolved.
4 Add the citric acid, tannin and pectin destroying enzyme to the pail. Cover it and leave for 24 hours.
5 Add the yeast and nutrient, then stand the pail in a warm place for three weeks.
6 Strain the must into a fermentation jar and seal it with an airlock.
7 When fermentation has ceased, rack the wine into a clean container with one crushed Campden tablet, and close the container with a bung or safety lock.
8 Rack every two month till clear.

Nettle wine

Classification: Table, Medium, White

INGREDIENTS	UK/US	METRIC
Nettles (tops only, young)	½ gallon	2.3 litres
Lemons, 1		
Ginger root, 1 piece		
Sugar	3lb	1.8kg
Citric acid	½oz	14g
Tannin, 2 to 3 drops or	$\frac{1}{16}$oz	1.75g
Yeast		
Yeast nutrient		
Campden tablets		

1 Wash the nettle tops, and allow them to drain.
2 Pare the zest from the lemons and squeeze out the juice.
3 Bruise the ginger root.
4 Put the nettles, lemon zest and juice and

the ginger root into a pan with water to cover them. Bring to the boil and simmer for 30 minutes.
5 Dissolve the sugar in a little hot water.
6 Strain the liquid from the pan into a pail, add the sugar syrup, citric acid and tannin.
7 Add warm water to make up to 1 gallon (4.5 litres), add the yeast and nutrient, cover the pail and stand it in a warm place, stirring daily.
8 After seven days, rack the must into a fermentation vessel and seal it with an airlock.
9 When fermentation is complete, rack the wine into a container, add one crushed Campden tablet and close the container with a bung or safety lock.
10 Rack every two months till clear.

Oakleaf wine

Classification: Table, Medium, White

INGREDIENTS	UK/US	METRIC
Oakleaves, green	1 gallon	4.5 litres
Lemons, 2		
Sugar	3½lb	1.59kg
Citric acid	¼oz	7g
Yeast, all-purpose		
Yeast nutrient		
Campden tablets		

1 Wash the leaves thoroughly and drain them.
2 Boil ¾ gallon (3.4 litres) of water and add

the sugar; stir until dissolved.

3 Put the leaves into a pail and pour the boiling liquid over them. Cover and leave to stand for 24 hours.

4 Squeeze the juice from the lemons; add this juice and the citric acid to the pail and stir well.

5 Strain into a fermentation vessel and add the yeast and nutrient, and warm water to make up to 1 gallon (4.5 litres).

6 Seal the vessel with an airlock and stand it in a warm place.

7 When fermentation is complete, rack the wine into a clean container, add one crushed Campden tablet, and seal the container with a bung or safety lock.

8 Rack every two months till clear.

Orange & sultana wine

Classification: Dessert, Sweet*, White

INGREDIENTS	UK/US	METRIC
Oranges, sweet, to make 2 pints juice		
Lemons, 2		
Sultanas (or white raisins)	1lb	454g
Sugar	4lb	1.8kg
Tannin, 2 to 3 drops or	$\frac{1}{16}$oz	1.75g
Yeast, all-purpose		
Yeast nutrient		
Campden tablets		
Pectin destroying enzyme		

1 Pare the zest from the oranges and lemons and squeeze out the juice.

2 Deseed and chop the sultanas, then put them into a pail with the orange and lemon juice.

3 Put the zest of the oranges and lemons into a small bowl, add $\frac{1}{2}$ pint (284ml) of boiling water and crush the zest with the back of a spoon. Allow to stand for an hour, then strain the liquid into the pail.

4 Dissolve the sugar and add the tannin and pectin destroying enzyme. Make up to 1 gallon (4.5 litres) then cover the pail and stand it in a warm place.

5 After 24 hours, add the yeast and nutrient.

6 After three more days, strain into a fermentation vessel and fit an airlock.

7 When fermentation is complete, rack into a clean container, add one crushed Campden tablet and close the container with a bung or safety lock.

8 Rack after two months, and again later if necessary.

Comment

If the wine is made without the orange and lemon zest, a rather tasteless result is produced. This would serve excellently as the wine basis for an orange liqueur, however.

*For a dry wine use 2½lb (1.13kg) sugar.

Parsnip wine

Classification: Table, Medium, White

INGREDIENTS	UK/US	METRIC
Parsnips	5lb	2.27kg
Lemon, 1		

	UK/US	METRIC
Sugar	3lb	1.36kg
Citric acid	$\frac{1}{2}$oz	14g
Tannin, 2 to 3 drops or	$\frac{1}{16}$oz	1.75g
Yeast, all-purpose		
Yeast nutrient		
Campden tablets		
Pectin destroying enzyme		

1 Wash and peel the parsnips, cut them into small pieces and boil them until tender in 1 gallon (4.5 litres) of water.
2 Strain off the water into a pail, but do not squeeze or press the parsnips, or the wine will be cloudy.
3 Pare the lemon to remove the zest, and squeeze out the juice.
4 Add the lemon zest and juice, the citric acid, pectin destroying enzyme, tannin and a crushed Campden tablet to the pail.
5 Dissolve the sugar in a little hot water and add the syrup to the pail. Allow it to stand for 24 hours.
6 Add the yeast and nutrient, stir well, cover the pail and stand it in a warm place,
7 Stir daily; after 2 weeks, strain the must into a fermentation jar and seal it with an airlock.
8 When fermentation is complete, rack the wine into a clean container, add one crushed Campden tablet and close the container with a bung or safety lock.
9 Rack after two months and again before bottling.

Peach (canned) wine

Classification: Table, Medium, White

INGREDIENTS	UK/US	METRIC
Canned peach halves, slices or pulp	2lb	907g
Sugar	2$\frac{1}{2}$lb	1.13kg
Citric acid	$\frac{1}{2}$oz	14g
Tannin, 2 to 3 drops or	$\frac{1}{16}$oz	1.75g
Yeast, all-purpose		
Yeast nutrient		
Campden tablets		
Pectin destroying enzyme		

1 If the peaches are in halves or pieces, cut them up.
2 Boil a kettleful of water and dissolve the sugar to form a syrup.
3 Mix together the sugar syrup, the syrup from the peach can, and the peaches, in a pail, then add $\frac{3}{4}$ gallon (3.4 litres) of hot water. Stir well.
4 Add the citric acid, tannin and pectin destroying enzyme. Stir again, cover and stand the mixture in a warm place for 24 hours.
5 Add the yeast and nutrient, stir, cover and stand it in a warm place, stirring daily for 10 days.
6 Strain the must into a fermentation jar and seal this with an airlock.
7 When fermentation is complete, rack the wine into a clean container, add one crushed Campden tablet and close the container with a bung or safety lock.
8 Rack after two months, and again before bottling.

Pea pod wine

Classification: Table, Medium, White

INGREDIENTS	UK/US	METRIC
Pea pods, young	4$\frac{1}{2}$lb	2kg
Sugar	3lb	1.36kg
Citric acid	$\frac{1}{4}$oz	7g
Tannin, 2 to 3 drops or	$\frac{1}{16}$oz	1.75g
Yeast		

Yeast nutrient
Campden tablets
Pectin destroying
enzyme

1 Wash and drain the pea pods.
2 Put the pea pods into a pan, add a crushed Campden tablet and 1 gallon (4.5 litres) of water and boil until the pods are tender.
3 Strain the water into a pail and add the sugar, citric acid, tannin and pectin destroying enzyme.
4 Stir thoroughly until the sugar has dissolved. Allow to stand for 24 hours.
5 Add the yeast and nutrient, stir again, cover the pail and stand it in a warm place.
6 Stir daily; after three days, strain the must into a fermentation jar and seal it with an airlock.
7 When fermentation is complete, rack the wine into a clean container, add one crushed Campden tablet and close it with a bung or safety lock.
8 Rack every two months till clear.

Pineapple (canned) wine

Classification: Table, Medium to dry, White

1 Proceed exactly as for Peach (canned) Wine, but substituting 2lb (907g) canned pineapple slices or chunks.

Plum wine

Classification: Table, Medium, Rosé

INGREDIENTS	UK/US	METRIC
Plums, red or black, ripe	6lb	2.7kg
Sugar	3lb	1.36kg

Citric acid	$\frac{1}{4}$oz	7g
Tannin, 2 to 3 drops or	$\frac{1}{16}$oz	1.75g
Yeast, all-purpose		
Yeast nutrient		
Campden tablets		
Pectin destroying enzyme		

1 Wash the fruit thoroughly and drain it.
2 Place the fruit in 1 gallon (4.5 litres) of boiling water and simmer it for 10 minutes, then transfer to a pail.
3 Add the sugar, citric acid, tannin, a crushed Campden tablet and the pectin destroying enzyme. Stir until the sugar has dissolved. Leave for 24 hours, covered.
4 Add the yeast and nutrient, stir well, cover the pail and stand it in a warm place, stirring daily.
5 After three days, strain into a fermentation vessel and fit an airlock.
6 When fermentation is complete, rack the wine into a container, add one crushed Campden tablet and close it with a bung or safety lock.
7 Rack every two months till clear.

Pomegranate & barley wine

Classification: Table, Medium, White

INGREDIENTS	UK/US	METRIC
Pomegranates, 10		
Barley	8oz	227g
Lemon, 1		
Sugar	3lb	1.36kg
Citric acid	$\frac{1}{2}$oz	14g
Tannin, 2 to 3 drops or	$\frac{1}{16}$oz	1.75g
Yeast, cereal-type		
Yeast nutrient		
Campden tablets		
Pectin destroying enzyme		

1 Put the barley in a pan with ½ gallon (2.3 litres) of water, bring it slowly to the boil and simmer for 5 minutes.
2 Split open the pomegranates and scrape the seeds into a pail.
3 Squeeze the juice from the lemon and add this juice, the citric acid, tannin, pectin destroying enzyme and sugar to the pail.
4 Strain the water from the barley into the pail and stir until the sugar has dissolved.
5 Make up the mixture with warm water to 1 gallon (4.5 litres) and stand for 24 hours. Add the yeast and nutrient.
6 Cover the pail and stand it in a warm place for five days, stirring daily.
7 At the end of this period strain into a fermentation vessel and seal with an airlock.
8 When fermentation is complete, rack the wine into a clean container, add one crushed Campden tablet and close it with a bung or safety lock.
9 Rack every two months till clear.

Pyment

Classification: Table, Medium, White

INGREDIENTS	UK/US	METRIC
Grape juice concentrate, ½ can	1lb 2oz	510g
Honey (pale)	2½lb	1.13kg
Yeast, all-purpose		
Yeast nutrient		
Campden tablets		

1 Dissolve the honey in hot water and simmer for 5 minutes, then pour directly into the fermentation vessel.
2 Add the grape concentrate then add warm water to make up to 1 gallon (4.5 litres). Stir well.
3 Add the yeast and nutrient, seal the fermentation vessel with an airlock and stand it in a warm place.
4 When fermentation is complete, rack the wine into a clean container, add one crushed Campden tablet and close the container with a bung or safety lock.
5 Rack every two months for six months, then less frequently as sediment forms.

Comment
If fresh grapes are available, press the juice from 3lb (1.36kg), and increase the honey to 3½ lb (1.59kg).

Raspberry wine

Classification: Table, Medium, Rosé

INGREDIENTS	UK/US	METRIC
Raspberries, ripe	4lb	1.8kg
Sugar	3½lb	1.59kg
Citric acid	¼oz	7g
Yeast, all-purpose		
Yeast nutrient		
Campden tablets		
Pectin destroying enzyme		

1 Wash the raspberries gently and drain them.
2 Put the fruit into a pail, add ¾ gallon (3.4 litres) of boiling water and crush the fruit completely.

3 Cover the pail and leave it for four days, stirring daily.
4 Dissolve the sugar in a little hot water, then add this syrup, the citric acid and pectin destroying enzyme.
5 Add warm water to make up to 1 gallon (4.5 litres). After 24 hours add the yeast and nutrient; cover the pail and stand it in a warm place.
6 After two days, strain the liquid into a fermentation vessel and seal this with an airlock.
7 When fermentation is complete, rack the wine into a clean container, add one crushed Campden tablet and close the container with a bung or safety lock.
8 Rack after two months, and before bottling.

Rhubarb wine

Classification: Table, Medium, Rosé

INGREDIENTS	UK/US	METRIC
Rhubarb (red and ripe, but not the pink forced early rhubarb)	6lb	2.7kg
Lemons, 2		
Sugar	3½lb	1.59kg
Tannin, 2 to 3 drops or	$\frac{1}{16}$oz	1.75g
Yeast, all-purpose		
Yeast nutrient		
Campden tablets		
Pectin destroying enzyme		
Precipitated chalk	½oz	14g

1 Discard all the rhubarb leaves, which are poisonous.
2 Wash the rhubarb and drain it, cut it up into small pieces, crush it in a pail and cover it with ¾ gallon (3.4 litres) of cold water.

3 Add a crushed Campden tablet, stir this in, and leave for three days.
4 Strain the juice into a second pail and add the precipitated chalk. The wine will fizz as excess oxalic acid is neutralized.
5 Pare the zest from the lemons and squeeze out the juice.
6 Add the lemon zest and juice, the tannin and the pectin destroying enzyme to the pail.
7 Dissolve the sugar in a little hot water and add the syrup to the other ingredients. Make up to 1 gallon (4.5 litres) with water.
8 After 24 hours add the yeast and nutrient, cover the pail and stand it in a warm place. Stir daily.
9 After three days, strain it into a fermentation vessel and seal this with an airlock.
10 When fermentation is complete, rack the wine into a container, add one crushed Campden tablet and seal the container with a bung or safety lock.
11 Rack every two months till clear.

Rhubarb & beetroot (beet) wine

Classification: Table, Medium, Red

INGREDIENTS	UK/US	METRIC
Rhubarb	3lb	1.36kg
Beetroot (beet)	3lb	1.36kg
Whole wheat grains	1lb	454g
Raisins	8oz	227g
Sugar	3lb	1.8kg
Tannin, 2 to 3 drops or	$\frac{1}{16}$oz	1.75g
Yeast, cereal-type		
Yeast nutrient		
Ginger root, 1 piece		

Campden tablets		
Pectin destroying enzyme		
Precipitated chalk	$\frac{1}{2}$oz	14g

1 Cut the rhubarb into small pieces, discarding all leaves, which are poisonous.
2 Put the rhubarb into a pail and pour $\frac{1}{2}$ gallon (2.3 litres) of boiling water over it.
3 Sprinkle the precipitated chalk over the rhubarb; it will fizz, releasing excess oxalic acid.
4 Add one crushed Campden tablet and allow it to stand for 10 days, stirring and pressing the rhubarb every day, then strain it into a second pail.
5 Slice the beetroot, unpeeled, into $\frac{1}{2}$ gallon (2.3 litres) of hot water. When soft (in about 2 days), strain into the pail with the rhubarb juice.
6 Deseed and chop the raisins, 'bruise' the root ginger and add with the wheat, pectin destroying enzyme, tannin, sugar and raisins to the pail. Stir well to dissolve the sugar.
7 After 24 hours add the yeast and nutrient, then cover the pail and allow the must to ferment for four to five days, stirring daily.
8 Strain the liquid into a fermentation vessel and fit an airlock.
9 When fermentation is complete, rack into a clean container, add one crushed Campden tablet, and close the container with a bung or safety lock.
10 Rack every two months till clear.

Rice & raisin wine

Classification: Table, Medium, White

INGREDIENTS	UK/US	METRIC
Rice (unpolished or paddy)	1lb	454g
Raisins	1lb	454g
Lemon, 1		
Sugar	3lb	1.36kg
Tannin, 2 to 3 drops or	$\frac{1}{16}$oz	1.75g
Yeast, cereal-type		
Yeast nutrient		
Campden tablets		

1 Chop and deseed the raisins.
2 Pare the zest from the lemon, and squeeze out the juice.
3 Put the rice, chopped deseeded raisins, tannin, zest and juice of the lemon into a pail and add 1 gallon (4.5 litres) of boiling water.
4 Add the sugar and stir well until dissolved.
5 Add the yeast and nutrient, stir again, cover the pail and stand it in a warm place. Stir daily.
6 After seven days, strain the must into a fermentation vessel and seal it with an airlock.
7 When fermentation is complete, rack the wine into a clean container, add one crushed Campden tablet and close it with a bung or safety lock.
8 Rack every two months till clear.

Rose hip wine

Classification: Table, Medium, Rosé

INGREDIENTS	UK/US	METRIC
Rose hips, fully ripe	6 pints	3.4 litres
Orange, 1		
Sugar	3lb	1.36kg
Citric acid	$\frac{1}{2}$oz	14g
Tannin, 2 to 3 drops or	$\frac{1}{16}$oz	1.75g
Yeast, all-purpose		
Yeast nutrient		
Campden tablets		
Pectin destroying enzyme		

1 Wash the rose hips, drain, then crush them with a wooden mallet.
2 Place the hips in a pail and add ¾ gallon (3.4 litres) of boiling water.
3 Pare the zest from the orange and squeeze out the juice.
4 Add one crushed Campden tablet, and the zest and juice of the orange, to the pail. Allow it to stand for 24 hours.
5 Dissolve the sugar in a little hot water and add the syrup to the pail.
6 Add the citric acid, tannin, and pectin destroying enzyme. Stir well and cover the pail.
7 After 24 hours, add the yeast and nutrient. Stand the pail in a warm place for three days.
8 Make up the must to one gallon with warm water, strain into a fermentation vessel and seal this with an airlock.
9 When fermentation is complete, rack the wine into a clean container, add one crushed Campden tablet, and close the container with a bung or safety lock.
10 Rack every two months, for six months, then less frequently as sediment forms.

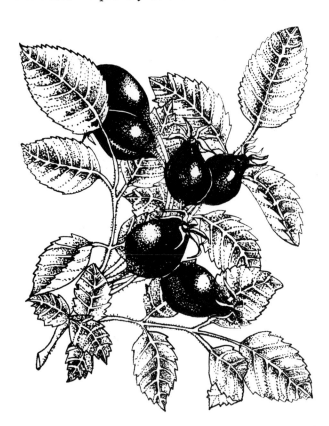

Rose petal wine

Classification: Table, Medium, White

INGREDIENTS	UK/US	METRIC
Rose petals (red, scented are best)	4 pints	2.3 litres
Sultanas (or white raisins)	6oz	170g
Lemon, 1		
Orange, 1		
Sugar	3lb	1.36kg
Citric acid	¼oz	7g
Tannin, 2 to 3 drops or	$\frac{1}{16}$oz	1.75g
Yeast, all-purpose		
Yeast nutrient		
Campden tablets		

1 Wash the petals thoroughly.
2 Pare the zest from the orange and lemon, and squeeze out the juice.
3 Chop and deseed the sultanas.
4 Add together in a pail the rose petals, sugar, orange and lemon zest and juice, and the sultanas. Cover these with 1 gallon (4.5 litres) of boiling water.
5 Stir well to dissolve the sugar.
6 When lukewarm, add the citric acid, tannin yeast and nutrient.
7 Cover the pail and stand it in a warm place, stirring daily.
8 After seven days, strain the must into a fermentation vessel, and seal this with an airlock.
9 When fermentation is complete, rack the wine into a storage container, add one crushed Campden tablet and close the container with a bung or safety lock.
10 Rack every two months, for six months, then less frequently as sediment forms.

Sangria is a popular summer drink.

Sangria

Classification: Summer cup

INGREDIENTS	UK/US	METRIC
Red or white wine, 2 bottles		
Orange, 1		
Lemon, 1		
Sugar	8oz	227g

1 Slice the orange and lemon thinly, and place half of each in two glass jugs, about 3 hours before the Sangria will be required.
2 Add the wine to the fruit — one jug of white and one of red looks attractive on the table.
3 Taste before serving — if required, add a little sugar and stir well.
4 Finally, add a few ice cubes.

'Sherry' wine

Classification: Aperitif, Medium, Red

INGREDIENTS	UK/US	METRIC
Sherry grape juice concentrate, 1 can	2lb 3oz	1kg
Sugar	12oz	340g
Yeast, all-purpose*		
Yeast nutrient		
Campden tablets		
Vodka, 100° proof	3fl oz	85ml

1 Proceed exactly as the Vin Ordinaire recipe.
2 When the wine is matured it will have a sherry flavour, but real sherry is fortified.
3 If you like what you have made, put 3fl oz (85ml) of 100° proof Vodka into a wine bottle and fill it with the 'sherry'. Seal the bottle and leave it for a few days before use.

Comment
*Sherry-type cultured yeast could be tried for this recipe.

Sloe wine

Classification: Dessert, Sweet, Red

INGREDIENTS	UK/US	METRIC
Sloes	3½lb	1.59kg
Raisins	8oz	227g
Sugar	3½lb	1.59kg
Yeast, all-purpose		
Yeast nutrient		
Campden tablets		
Pectin destroying enzyme		

1 Wash the sloes gently and drain them.
2 Put the sloes into a pail and cover them with ¾ gallon (3.4 litres) of boiling water. Cover the pail with a cloth.

IAN REID

3 Let the sloes soak for a day, then mash them well.

4 Chop and deseed the raisins, and add them and the pectin destroying enzyme to the pail.

5 Dissolve the sugar in a little boiling water, and add this to the pail. Add a further $\frac{1}{4}$ gallon (1.14 litres) of hot water and stir well. Stand for 24 hours.

6 Add the yeast and nutrient, cover the pail and stand it in a warm place.

7 After 10 days, strain the must into a fermentation vessel and seal this with an airlock.

8 When fermentation is complete, rack the wine into a container, add one crushed Campden tablet and close the container with a bung or safety lock.

9 Rack every two months, for six months, then less frequently as sediment forms.

Strawberry wine

Classification: Table, Medium*, Rosé

INGREDIENTS	UK/US	METRIC
Strawberries, ripe	4lb	1.8kg
Sugar	3lb	1.36kg
Citric acid	$\frac{1}{2}$oz	$\frac{1}{4}$g
Tannin,		
2 to 3 drops or	$\frac{1}{16}$oz	1.75g
Yeast, all-purpose		
Yeast nutrient		
Campden tablets		
Pectin destroying enzyme		

1 Hull the strawberries, wash them well and allow them to drain.

2 Dissolve the sugar in a little hot water, add the strawberries and mash them thoroughly.

3 Add $\frac{1}{2}$ gallon (2.3 litres) of warm water and leave in a covered pail for two days.

4 Add the citric acid, tannin and pectin destroying enzyme. Stand for 24 hours.

5 Add a further $\frac{1}{2}$ gallon (2.3 litres) of warm

Strawberries make a delicious dry wine.

water, stir well and strain into the fermentation vessel.

6 Add the yeast and yeast nutrient, and seal the vessel with an airlock.

7 When fermentation is complete, strain the must into a container, add one crushed Campden tablet and close the container with a bung or safety lock.

8 Rack after two months and again before bottling.

Comment
*Makes an excellent dry wine using 2½lb (1.13kg) of sugar.

Tea & raisin wine

Classification: Table, Medium dry, White

INGREDIENTS	UK/US	METRIC
Raisins	2lb	907g
Whole wheat grains	1lb	454g
Tea (dry)	1oz	28g
Lemons, 4		
Sugar	2lb	907g
Citric acid	½oz	14g
Yeast, cereal-type		
Yeast nutrient		
Campden tablets		

1 Put the tea into a jug and pour 1 pint (568ml) of boiling water over it. Let it stand until cold, then strain the liquid into a pail.

2 Chop and deseed the raisins and squeeze the juice from the lemons.

3 Add the raisins and lemon juice to the pail, with the wheat, citric acid and the sugar.

4 Add ¾ gallon (3.4 litres) of hot water to the pail and stir well until the sugar is dissolved.

5 Add the yeast and nutrient, cover the pail and stand it in a warm place for 21 days, stirring daily.

6 Strain into a fermentation vessel, make up to 1 gallon (4.5 litres) with water and seal this with an airlock.

7 When fermentation is complete, rack the wine into a clean container, add one crushed Campden tablet and close it with a bung or safety lock.

8. Rack every two months till clear.

Vermouth wine

Classification: Aperitif, Medium, White or red

INGREDIENTS	UK/US	METRIC
Vermouth grape concentrate, 1 can	2lb 3oz	1kg
Sugar as called for on can		
Yeast, all-purpose*		
Yeast nutrient		
Campden tablets		

Method 1
1 Proceed exactly as for Vin Ordinaire.

Method 2
1 Use one can of white grape juice concentrate, but obtain the vermouth flavour herbs separately: when fermented out, put some herbs in a muslin (cheese cloth) bag and steep them in a little of the wine for two or three days. Add this back to the wine and taste. If the flavour is not strong enough, steep the herbs in the same manner for a few more days.

Comment
Real Vermouth is a fortified wine. Both of the above wines will have a Vermouth flavour and can be drunk as they are, or fortified by the addition of 3 fl oz (85 ml) of 100° proof vodka per bottle. But make sure that you like the wine before adding the spirit.

*Vermouth-type cultured yeast could be used for this recipe.

Vin ordinaire

Classification: Table, Dry, Red, rose or white

INGREDIENTS	UK/US	METRIC
Grape juice concentrate of the desired type, 1 can	2lb 3oz	1kg
Sugar	10oz	284g
Yeast, all-purpose		
Yeast nutrient		
Campden tablets		

1 Bring a kettleful of water almost to boiling point.
2 Empty the can of juice into a jug. Dissolve completely all the residue in the can with hot water, and add this to the jug.
3 Empty the contents into a 1 gallon (4.5 litres) fermentation vessel.
4 Fill the vessel three-quarters full (i.e. make up to 6 pints or 3.4 litres) with warm water.
5 Add the yeast and nutrient.
6 Fit an airlock and stand the vessel in a warm place.
7 After 10 days fermentation, dissolve half the sugar in a little hot water. Add the resulting syrup to the must.
8 After a further five days dissolve the remainder of the sugar in hot water and add this to the must, then fill the vessel up to 1 gallon (4.5 litres) with warm water.
9 When fermentation is complete (three to four weeks), rack into a clean container, add one crushed Campden tablet and close the container.

Comment
This is the easiest of all wines to make; many people make no other and have a regular system of starting a new ferment every fortnight or so, according to usage. It saves time and trouble to make two cans together.

If you like a weaker flavoured wine of the usual alcoholic strength, try making two gallons of wine from one can. That is, halve the concentrate, but use the same quantities given in the recipe for everything else.
If initially in doubt, follow the instructions on the label; adjustments to the quantity of sugar, if desired, can be made with a later batch.

Wheat wine

Classification: Table, Medium, White

INGREDIENTS	UK/US	METRIC
Whole wheat	1½lb	680g
Raisins	1lb	454g
Sultanas (or white raisins)	1lb	454g
Orange, 1		
Lemon, 1		
Grapefruit, 1		
Sugar	2½lb	1.13kg
Tannin, 2 to 3 drops or	$\frac{1}{16}$oz	1.75g
Yeast, cereal-type		
Yeast nutrient		
Campden tablets		

1 Crush the wheat in a mincer (grinder).
2 Chop and deseed the raisins and sultanas.
3 Pare the zest from the citrus fruit and squeeze out the juice.
4 Put the crushed wheat, raisins, sugar, sultanas, zest and juice of the fruit into a pail and pour 1 gallon (4.5 litres) of boiling water over them. Stir until the sugar has dissolved.
5 When lukewarm, add the tannin, yeast and nutrient.
6 Cover the pail and stand it in a warm place for seven days.
7 Strain the must into a fermentation vessel, and seal this with an airlock.
8 When fermentation is complete, rack the wine into a container, add one crushed Campden tablet and close the container with a bung or safety lock.
9 Rack every two months till clear.

Wine 16 Instant recipes

Instant blackcurrant wine

Classification: Dessert, Medium, Red

INGREDIENTS	UK/US	METRIC
Ribena (or other blackcurrant) syrup		
1 bottle	12fl oz	341ml
Sugar	1½lb	680g
Citric acid	¼oz	7g
Yeast, granulated		
Yeast nutrient		

1 Pour the syrup directly into the fermentation vessel.
2 Dissolve ½ lb (227g) of the sugar in hot water, and add this, with the citric acid, to the vessel.
3 Make up to 6 pints (3.4 litres) of must with warm water, add the yeast and nutrient, then seal the vessel with an airlock.
4 Stand the vessel in a warm place (70°F, 21°C), maintaining this temperature.
5 After three days, add half of the remaining sugar, in dissolved form.
6 After a further three days, add the remainder of the sugar, dissolved, and make the must up to 1 gallon (4.5 litres).
7 When fermentation has finished, in 14 to 21 days, rack off the wine.
8 Allow it to stand for at least seven days, then filter it as many times as is needed to clear it.

Comment
This wine will not keep; consume it within two weeks.

Instant burgundy wine

Classification: Table, Dry, Red

INGREDIENTS	UK/US	METRIC
Burgundy grape juice concentrate,		
1 can	2lb 3oz	1kg
Sugar	8oz	227g
Yeast, granulated		
Yeast nutrient		

1 Proceed exactly as for Instant Vin Ordinaire Wine.

Instant grapefruit wine

Classification: Table, Dry, White

INGREDIENTS	UK/US	METRIC
Grapefruit juice, 1 can, sweetened	1lb 3oz	538g
Sugar	1½lb	680g
Yeast, granulated		
Yeast nutrient		

1 Pour the juice straight into the fermentation vessel.
2 Dissolve ½ lb (227 g) of the sugar in hot water and add to the vessel. Add ¾ gallon water and the yeast and nutrient. Seal the vessel with an airlock.
3 Stand the vessel in a warm place (70°F, 21°C), maintaining this temperature.
4 After three days, add half of the remaining sugar, in dissolved form.
5 After a further three days, add the remainder of the sugar, dissolved, and make up to 1 gallon (4.5 litres).
6 When fermentation has finished — in about 21 days — rack off the wine.
7 Stand the wine for seven days, then filter it; two or more filterings may be necessary to clear the wine, which should now be drinkable.

Comment
This wine will not keep for long; consume it within two weeks.

Instant oakleaf wine

Classification: Table, Medium, White

INGREDIENTS	UK/US	METRIC
Oakleaves, green	1 gallon	4.5 litres
Lemons, 2		
Sugar	2½lb	1.13kg
Citric acid	¼oz	7g
Yeast, granulated		
Yeast nutrient		

1 Wash the leaves thoroughly and drain them.
2 Boil ¾ gallon (3.4 litres) of water and add 1½lb (680g) sugar; stir well until dissolved.
3 Put the leaves into a pail and pour boiling water over them; allow it to stand for 24 hours.
4 Squeeze the juice from the lemons; add this juice and the citric acid to the pail and stir well.
5 Strain into a fermentation vessel, then add the yeast and nutrient. Stir well and make up the must to 1 gallon (4.5 litres).
6 Seal the vessel with an airlock and stand it in a warm place (70°F, 21°C). Maintain this temperature.
7 After three days, add half of the remaining sugar, dissolved.
8 After a further three days, add the remaining 8 oz (227 g) of sugar, dissolved; if necessary make the must up to 1 gallon (4.5 litres).
9 When fermentation has finished, in 14 to 21 days, rack off the wine.
10 Allow it to stand for at least seven days, then filter it until clear.

Comment

This wine will not keep; consume it within two weeks.

Instant pea pod wine

Classification: Table, Medium dry, White

INGREDIENTS	UK/US	METRIC
Pea pods, young	$4\frac{1}{2}$lb	2kg
Sugar	2lb	907g
Citric acid	$\frac{1}{4}$oz	7g
Tannin, 2 to 3 drops or	$\frac{1}{16}$oz	1.75g
Yeast, granulated		
Yeast nutrient		
Campden tablets		
Pectin destroying enzyme		

1 Wash and drain the pea pods.
2 Put the pea pods into a pan with a crushed Campden tablet. Add 1 gallon (4.5 litres) of water and boil this until the pods are tender.
3 Strain the liquor into a fermentation vessel, dissolve all the sugar in warm water and add this to the vessel, together with the citric acid, tannin and pectin destroying enzyme.
4 Stir thoroughly, After 24 hours add the yeast and nutrient. Seal the vessel with an airlock.
5 Stand the vessel in a warm place (70°F, 21°C), maintaining this temperature.
6 When fermentation has finished (in 14 to 21 days) rack off the wine.
7 Allow the wine to stand for at least seven days, then filter it until clear.

Comment

This wine will not keep: consume it within two weeks.

Instant vin ordinaire

Classification: Table, Medium, Red, white or rosé

INGREDIENTS	UK/US	METRIC
Red, white or rosé grape juice concentrate, 1 can	2lb 3oz	1 kg
Sugar	8oz	227g
Yeast, granulated		
Yeast nutrient		

1 Pour the concentrate into a jug, rinsing out any juice from the can with very hot water.
2 Pour the contents of the jug into the fermentation vessel, then add warm water to make up to 6 pints (3.4 litres).
3 Dissolve half of the sugar in warm water and add this to the vessel; stir well, then add the yeast and yeast nutrient, and seal the vessel with an airlock.
4 Stand the vessel in a warm place (70°F, 21°C), maintaining this temperature.
5 After three days, add half of the remaining sugar, dissolved.
6 After a further three days, add the remaining 2 oz (57g) of sugar, dissolved, and make the total quantity of must up to 1 gallon with warm water.
7 Fermentation should finish in 14 to 21 days from commencement; when finished, rack off the wine.
8 Stand the wine for one week, then filter it repeatedly until clear.

Comment

This wine is intended for consumption within two weeks of clearing.